Slumdog Millionaire

Teacher's Guide
Frauke Vieregge

Ernst Klett Sprachen
Stuttgart

Every attempt has been made to contact copyright holders. Additions or corrections to the names and/or organisations printed herein will be welcomed.

Trotz entsprechender Bemühungen ist es nicht in allen Fällen gelungen, den Rechtsinhaber ausfindig zu machen. Berechtigte Ansprüche werden selbstverständlich im Rahmen der üblichen Vereinbarungen abgegolten.

Bildquellennachweis

Folie Imago, Berlin; S. 40 + 77 http://www.indiatalkies.com/2011/03/dandi-march-corruption-india.html; S. 60 + 61 Ullstein Bild GmbH (Roger Viollet), Berlin; S. 17 + 61 shutterstock (thefinalmiracle), New York, NY; S. 65 Thinkstock (Stockbyte), München; S. 66 Thinkstock (istockphoto), München; S. 34 + 72 www.cartoonstock.com (Kes), Bath; S. 34 + 72 Getty Images (INDRANIL MUKHERJEE/AFP), München; S. 43 + 80 Picture-Alliance (ABC Television Network/Entertainment Pictures ZPress), Frankfurt; S. 46 + 82 shutterstock (beboy), New York, NY; S. 46 + 82 Thinkstock (istockphoto), München; S. 84 shutterstock (Dario Diament), New York, NY

Sollte es in einem Einzelfall nicht gelungen sein, den korrekten Rechteinhaber ausfindig zu machen, so werden berechtigte Ansprüche selbstverständlich im Rahmen der üblichen Regelungen abgegolten.

1. Auflage   1 $^{6\ 5\ 4\ 3\ 2}$ | 2015 14 13 12 11

Die letzte Zahl bezeichnet das Jahr des Druckes. Das Werk und seine Teile sind urheberrechtlich geschützt. Jede Nutzung in anderen als den gesetzlich zugelassenen Fällen bedarf der vorherigen schriftlichen Einwilligung des Verlags. Hinweis zu § 52 a UrhG: Weder das Werk noch seine Teile dürfen ohne eine solche Einwilligung eingescannt und in ein Netzwerk eingestellt werden. Dies gilt auch für Intranets von Schulen und sonstigen Bildungseinrichtungen. Fotomechanische oder andere Wiedergabeverfahren nur mit Genehmigung des Verlags.

© Ernst Klett Sprachen GmbH, Rotebühlstraße 77, 70178 Stuttgart, 2011.
Alle Rechte vorbehalten.
Internetadresse: www.klett.de / www.lektueren.com

Autorin: Frauke Vieregge
Redaktion: Paul Newcomb
Layoutkonzeption: Elmar Feuerbach
Gestaltung und Satz: Swabianmedia, Stuttgart
Umschlaggestaltung: Elmar Feuerbach
Titelbild: iStockphoto (Krishna Somya), Calgary, Alberta
Illustrationen S. 86: Oliver Lucht
Druck und Bindung: AZ Druck und Datentechnik GmbH, Heisinger Straße 16, 87437 Kempten/Allgäu / Medienhaus Plump GmbH, Rolandsecker Weg 33, 53619 Rheinbreitbach
Printed in Germany
ISBN 978-3-12-579875-5

Inhaltsverzeichnis

Vorwort 4

I. Einführung
1.1 Zusammenfassung der Romanhandlung 5
1.2 Kompetenzen im Englischunterricht 6
1.3 Didaktische Konzeption 7
1.4 Online-Links 9
1.5 Synopsis 9

II. Module 1 The life of an Indian orphan
2.1 Einführung 14
2.2 The importance of a family 15
2.3 Life in the slums 22
2.4 Welfare organisations in India 23

III. Module 2 The lives of the whites in India
3.1 Einführung 24
3.2 Juvenile domestic servants 25
3.3 Racism against Indians in Australia 29

IV. Module 3 The dark side of India
4.1 Einführung 32
4.2 Police violence in India 33
4.3 Crime in India 36
4.4 Corruption in India 39

V. Module 4 The media in India
5.1 Einführung 42
5.2 Who Wants to Be a Millionaire? 43
5.3 The genre of Bollywood movies 44
5.4 The actors in Bollywood movies – hero and heroine 45
5.5 Indian woman – heroine, prostitute, worker 49

VI. Module 5 Slumdog Millionaire: the movie
6.1 Einführung 53
6.2 Tools for Film Analysis 54
6.3 *Slumdog Millionaire*, Chapter 1: The interrogation 55
6.4 *Slumdog Millionaire*, Chapter 4: being a professional beggar . 57

VII. Worksheets 60

VIII. Anhang
8.1 Brief history of modern India 93
6.2 Literaturverzeichnis 96

Vorwort

Mit der Akzeptanz des Gemeinsamen europäischen Referenzrahmens für Sprachen als Grundlage für Lehrpläne und für zentrale Prüfungen, sowie der Vereinbarung von nationalen Bildungsstandards, hat eine neue Ausrichtung des modernen Fremdsprachenunterrichts stattgefunden. Früher stand die Vermittlung landeskundlicher Inhalte und die Beherrschung der Fremdsprache im Vordergrund. Heute sollen die SuS eine transkulturelle Kompetenz erlangen, ebenso wie Sprachlernkompetenz und kommunikative Kompetenz. Dies bedeutet, dass die SuS unterschiedliche kulturelle Perspektiven respektieren und von ihnen lernen sollen, um ökologische und ökonomische Aspekte in einer globalisierten Welt erfassen zu können.

Im Rahmen der Sprachlernkompetenz liegt der Schwerpunkt nun auf selbst gesteuertem, kooperativem, reflektiertem Sprachlernen, im Bereich der kommunikativen Kompetenz stehen Hör- und Hör/Sehverstehen, Leseverstehen, Sprechen, Schreiben, und Sprachmittlung im Vordergrund. Der Unterricht ist lernerzentriert und stärker auf Inhalte ausgerichtet, die der unmittelbaren Erfahrungswelt der SuS entspringen. Das Kerncurriculum des niedersächsischen Kultusministeriums hat verschiedene Grundsätze bei der Auswahl von Lerninhalten festgelegt. Die Förderung der verschiedenen Kompetenzen soll durch authentisches und komplexes Sprachhandeln geschehen, auch wenn dies in der schulischen Situation meist nur simuliert werden kann. Komplexes und für die SuS bedeutsames Sprachhandeln ist auf entsprechende Inhalte angewiesen. Die Effektivität des Unterrichts hängt deshalb wesentlich von der Vernetzung der Kompetenzen und der Lerninhalte ab. Von besonderer Bedeutung für die Auswahl der Inhalte sind

- die lebenspraktische Relevanz der Inhalte und Methoden für die Lernenden,
- die Authentizität der eingesetzten Medien, Texte und Handlungsanlässe,
- die für den Zielsprachenraum relevanten kulturellen Bezüge,
- das in sprachlicher, methodischer und inhaltlicher Hinsicht weiterentwickelte Anspruchsniveau.

Ein wichtiges Ziel des Englischunterrichts ist, dass SuS authentische Texte unterschiedlicher Art und Länge weitgehend verstehen und die darin enthaltenen Informationen aufnehmen, einordnen und interpretieren können, doch auch muttersprachliche Texte sind im Sinne der Mediation und Sprachmittlung „erlaubt", um einen Perspektivwechsel zu ermöglichen. Zur Festigung der Lesekompetenz ist es erforderlich, grundlegende Lesestrategien (*skimming / careful / detailed reading, scanning*) und wörterbuchunabhängige Erschließungstechniken zu vermitteln und zu festigen.

I. Einführung

1.1 Zusammenfassung der Romanhandlung

Die Lektüre eines Romans aus einer anderen Kultur im Englischunterricht ermöglicht einerseits den LuL, die oben genannten Kompetenzen zu vermitteln, andererseits den SuS, sich mit der andersartigen Lebenssituation des Protagonisten auseinanderzusetzen und darüber in der Fremdsprache zu kommunizieren. Die Bearbeitung des Romans *Slumdog Millionaire* oder im Originaltitel *Q&A* („*Questions and Answers*") ermöglicht nicht nur eine schülerorientierte Lektüre, da der Protagonist im Alter der SuS ist, sondern auch die intensive Erarbeitung des landeskundlichen und sozio-kulturellen Themas „Indien".

Der 18-jährige Kellner Ram Mohammed Thomas hat in der indischen Version der Quizshow *Wer wird Millionär* alle zwölf Fragen richtig beantwortet und eine Milliarde Rupien – umgerechnet ca. 15 Millionen Euro – gewonnen. Er wusste die Antworten zu allen zwölf Fragen. Die Produktionsfirma der Quizshow hatte aber nie vor, das Preisgeld wirklich auszuzahlen und schon gar nicht an einen „Slumdog", ein Waisenkind ohne Schulbildung aus den Slums von Mumbai.

Die Produzenten werfen Thomas Betrug vor und halten die Ausstrahlung der Show zurück, solange die Sachlage unsicher ist, und Thomas wird festgenommen. Während des Verhörs bei der Polizei wird er gefoltert und nur das plötzliche Erscheinen einer Anwältin namens Smita, rettet ihn aus den Fängen der Polizeibeamten. In Vorbereitung einer Gerichtsverhandlung erzählt Thomas ihr in Rückblenden in zwölf Kapiteln seine Lebensgeschichte und die Ereignisse, die dazu geführt haben, dass er die zwölf Fragen wirklich mit Hilfe seines Wissens und seiner Lebenserfahrung richtig beantworten konnte: seine Rettung als Waisenkind durch die katholische Kirche, seine Kindheit bei einem Priester, sein Leben als Diener und seine Tätigkeit als Fremdenführer am Taj Mahal, um nur ein paar Abschnitte zu erwähnen.

Der Autor Vikas Swarup benutzt die zwölf Fragen der Quizshow als Leitfaden für die Darstellung von Thomas' Biographie. Thematisiert werden in den zwölf Kapiteln des Romans u. a. ethnische Spannungen zwischen Hindus, Moslems und Christen, Kinderarbeit, Korruption und die soziale Schere zwischen Arm und Reich. Thomas schlägt sich trotz mangelnder Bildung mit Glück und Geschick durchs Leben. Parallel zur Dramaturgie der Quizshow steigert sich die Romanhandlung von Kapitel zu Kapitel. Bei aller Tragik und Traurigkeit behält Thomas seinen Lebenswillen und seinen Humor. Er hält Kontakt zu seinem besten Freund Salim, der von einer Karriere als Bollywood-Schauspieler träumt, und er findet seine große Liebe in der Prostituierten Nita. Der Roman endet damit, dass die Anwältin ihm zu seinem Geld verhilft, womit er Nita freikaufen und heiraten kann. Sein Freund Salim wird ein Bollywood-Filmstar, und die Quizshow-Betreiber gehen Pleite.

Der Originaltitel der Lektüre ist „Q & A" (*Questions and Answers*); der neue Titel wurde der Lektüre nach dem großen Erfolg des gleichnamigen Films verliehen. Das Drehbuch des Films hat die Romanhandlung nur in Auszügen adaptiert und, der

Text wurde zugunsten der Publikumswirksamkeit sehr stark verändert. In Modul 4 wird deutlich, dass sich nur wenige Szenen des Filmes mit der Romanhandlung vergleichen lassen. Es bleibt der Lehrkraft überlassen, wie stark sie die Analyse des Films in die Unterrichtseinheit einfließen lässt. Obwohl die britische Ausgabe des DVDs zu empfehlen ist, reicht jedoch die deutschsprachige Version auch für die Analyse der hier vorgeschlagenen Szenen und deren Vergleich mit dem Buch ist aus. Ein wichtiges Entscheidungskriterium sind natürlich Untertitel auf Englisch.

1.2 Kompetenzen im Englischunterricht

Einstellungen entwickeln

Das Leben des Protagonisten Ram Mohammed Thomas ist von der indischen Kultur beeinflusst, einer Kultur, die den SuS mehrheitlich völlig fremd sein dürfte. *Slumdog Millionaire* ist für eine Studie über Indien insofern geeignet, als das viele Aspekte des indischen Alltags in die Romanhandlung einbezogen werden: die Filmindustrie des Bollywood-Movies mit seinen Darstellern, die vom Zuschauer vergöttert werden, die Lebensumstände in einem Slum und das Leben von Waisenkindern in einem Dritte-Welt-Land. Die SuS erschließen die Romanhandlung aus der westlichen Perspektive und müssen diese Perspektive verändern, um die Handlung des Romans verstehen und Geschehnisse einordnen zu können. Hilfestellung zum Verständnis erhalten die SuS durch Zusatzinformationen in verschiedenen Sekundärtexten und nicht zuletzt durch den Aufbau der Unterrichtseinheit in Modulen. Nur durch die Vertiefung der einzelnen Themen können die SuS die Romanhandlung umfassend verstehen und in ihren kulturellen Zusammenhang einordnen.

Fertigkeiten und Kompetenzen vertiefen

Das Anforderungsniveau der Lektüre entspricht in etwa dem B2/C1 des Gemeinsamen europäischen Referenzrahmens für Sprachen. In der gymnasialen Oberstufe haben die SuS die vier Kompetenzen, Lesen, Hören, Sprechen und Schreiben ausreichend trainiert. Diese Fertigkeiten müssen nicht mehr geübt, sondern nur noch vertieft werden. Auch in der Erarbeitung eines Lektüretextes muss den SuS Strategien vermittelt werden, um ihre individuellen Kompetenzen zu verbessern. Da in der Oberstufe Präsentationen in verschiedenen Formen und mit Hilfe verschiedenster Technik üblich sind, ist die kommunikative Kompetenz diejenige, die besonders trainiert werden muss, um den SuS einen sicheren Umgang mit der Methode der Präsentation zu ermöglichen. Die SuS haben in der gymnasialen Oberstufe Erfahrungen im Umgang mit authentischen Sachtexten, Graphiken und Tabellen und können diesen Materialien Informationen entnehmen, ordnen und gewichten. Diese Fertigkeiten werden durch die Materialien in diesem Lehrerheft ebenfalls vertieft und gefestigt.

> In Hamburg besteht die mündliche Abiturprüfung seit 2011 aus einer Präsentation.

Im Bereich der mündlichen Kommunikation wird erwartet, dass die Schüler relativ flüssig zu den im Unterricht behandelten Themen Stellung nehmen und sich an Gesprächen und Diskussionen auf der Grundlage eines zuvor vermittelten Repertoires an Redemitteln aktiv beteiligen und ihre eigene Meinung begründet vertreten. Die Beherrschung dieser Fertigkeit kann in der Oberstufe erwartet werden.

1.3 Didaktische Konzeption

Das hier vorgestellte Unterrichtsmodell ist modular aufgebaut und nach Unterrichtseinheiten strukturiert. Zu jedem Modul werden konkrete inhaltsbezogene Lernziele vorgestellt, Angaben zur jeweiligen Unterrichtsmethode bzw. zu Lernverfahren formuliert und Lösungsvorschläge (*Erwartungshorizonte*) skizziert. Im Anhang befinden sich in den **Kopiervorlagen** Worksheets, die methodisch unterschiedlich aufgebaut sind und somit nicht nur die verschiedenen Kompetenzen vertiefen, sondern auch die Möglichkeit bieten, die Unterrichtseinheit abwechslungsreich zu gestalten. Die Lektüre des Romans muss zu Beginn der Unterrichtseinheit nicht abgeschlossen sein, da sich die Module auf einzelne Kapitel beziehen und die SuS für die erfolgreiche Einzelbearbeitung nicht den gesamten Lektüretext kennen müssen. Selbstverständlich können auch einzelne Module weggelassen werden. Durch die Unabhängigkeit der Module voneinander müssen sie auch nicht chronologisch bearbeitet werden. Bei Zeitnot können z. B. die Module 3 und 4 weggelassen werden bzw. LuL sie in Referatform durch einzelne SuS erarbeiten zu lassen. Eine derartige „Reduzierung" empfiehlt sich insbesondere für Lerngruppen, die noch Probleme bei der Bewältigung von umfangreichen Ganzschriften haben.

Die Arbeit mit dem Roman wird ergänzt durch verschiedene thematische Einheiten, die alle das Thema „Indien" als Oberthema haben. **Modul 1** konzentriert sich auf das Leben von Waisenkindern in Indien. Der Protagonist des Romans ist Waise und der Roman stellt verschiedene Stationen seines Lebens ohne Eltern dar: bei dem katholischen Priester, in Jugendheimen, als Kinderbettler und als Hausangestellter sowohl bei einer australischen Diplomatenfamilie als auch bei einer Bollywood-Diva. In Modul 1 wird auch die Gefühlsebene der SuS angesprochen, indem sie persönliche Äußerungen zum Thema Familie tätigen und Bilder von Waisen interpretieren sollen. Auch die Thematik der Kinderbettler spricht die Emotionen der SuS an. Die Romanhandlung wird mit Zusatzinformationen verknüpft und somit ein breiteres Wissen über die Lebensrealität indischer Waisen erlangt. Die so geschaffene emotionale Basis wird genutzt, um die SuS eine Präsentation erarbeiten zu lassen über die Arbeit von NGOs, deren Ziel es ist, die Lebensumstände von indischen Waisen zu verbessern. Diese Arbeitsphase ist frei zu gestalten, da die SuS ihre Kompetenzen der Recherche und Präsentation selbständig anwenden sollen.

In **Modul 2** steht das Verhältnis von Weißen und der indischen Bevölkerung im Vordergrund. Besonderen Fokus wird auf das Thema der Kinderarbeit gelegt. Der Protagonist ist im Kapitel 50,000 Rupees Hausangestellter bei einer australischen Diplomatenfamilie, hieraus ergibt sich eine Reduktion des Themas Kinderarbeit auf genau diesen Teilbereich. Mithilfe von Sekundärtexten erarbeiten die SuS die gegenwärtige Situation von minderjährigen Hausangestellten und nehmen auf die Romanhandlung Bezug. Im Zusammenhang mit Modul 2 lässt sich auch die Einstellung von (meist vorübergehend dort wohnenden) Weißen gegenüber der (einheimischen) indischen Bevölkerung erarbeiten. Hierzu werden nicht nur englischsprachige Sekundärtext genutzt, sondern auch deutsche Texte sind möglich. Durch die Methode der Mediation kann besonders gut eine interkulturelle Perspektivveränderung bewirkt werden. Durch das Zusammenfassen eines deutschen Textes in englischer Sprache werden verschiedene Ebenen der

Sprachkompetenz gefordert: die korrekte Verwendung des Vokabulars bei der Übersetzung sowie die Vermittlung der kulturellen Besonderheiten bei der Inhaltsangabe des Textes. Das Medium des Blog ist relativ neu und sollte bei den SuS auf Interesse stoßen, zumal ihnen Blogs nicht unbekannt sein dürften.

In **Modul 3** wird das Thema Kriminalität mit der Methode der Tabellen- und Graphikanalyse erschlossen. Statistiken entschlüsseln zu können ist eine Fertigkeit, die im Gegensatz zu den anderen bislang erwähnten Kompetenzen eventuell noch gefestigt werden muss. Die SuS arbeiten mit verschiedenen Statistiken und Schaubildern und setzen sie in Bezug zur Handlung des Romans, der in mehreren Kapiteln das Thema Kriminalität behandelt: von Kinderbettlern über Überfälle in Zügen bis hin zu einem Auftragskiller. Eine kritische Stellungnahme der SuS wird durch Sekundärtexte zum Abschluss des Moduls ermöglicht.

Modul 4 umfasst das Thema „Bollywood", welches im Roman von Salim, dem Freund von Thomas repräsentiert wird. Die SuS arbeiten methodisch verstärkt mit der Bildanalyse und verknüpfen wiederum das Wissen aus Sekundärtexten mit der Handlung des Romans. Sie werden die Unterschiede in der Rezeption von Kinofilmen zwischen Deutschland und Indien kennenlernen und verstehen. Auch in diesem Modul liegt der Schwerpunkt auf der Festigung der Methode der Präsentation, einer Methode, bei welcher verschiedene Kompetenzen für ein erfolgreiches Ergebnis miteinander verknüpft werden müssen.

Den Abschluss der Unterrichtseinheit bildet der Vergleich des Filmes *Slumdog Millionaire* mit dem Roman in **Modul 5**. Es werden exemplarisch zwei Ausschnitte aus dem Film mit dem Lektüretext verglichen, um den SuS zu verdeutlichen, wie groß die Veränderungen von Roman zum Drehbuch sind. Die SuS sollen zu diesen Veränderungen kritisch Stellung nehmen und erkennen, dass die Publikumswirkung oftmals wichtiger ist als die Nähe zur Vorlage. Es sollte bei der Bearbeitung dieses Moduls unbedingt darauf geachtet werden, den englischen Film zu verwenden, da bei der deutschen Übersetzung viel von der Authentizität und besonders der Sprache verloren geht. Die beiden hier ausgewählten Textstellen können selbstverständlich um weitere ergänzt werden, welche dann mit dem Film verglichen werden.

Den Abschluss der Unterrichtsreihe bilden zwei von den Modulen unabhängige Klausurvorschläge, die sich auf die Romanhandlung als Ganzes stützen. Diese befinden sich auf den Seiten 68 bzw. 84 (Worksheets 5 bzw. 18). Die SuS sollten bis zum Ende dieser Unterrichtseinheit den Roman vollständig gelesen haben, um die hier vorliegenden Klausuren bewältigen zu können.

1.4 Online-Links

Einige Zusatzinformationen – und Artikel –, auf die dieses Lehrerhandbuch hinweist, sind natürlich im Internet. Wenn dies der Fall ist, finden Sie im Text einen Online-Link. Geben Sie den gesamten Code in das Suchfeld auf www.klett.de ein und Sie landen bei Listen, die Ihnen nützliche Links präsentieren.

I. Einführung

1.5 Synopsis

The plot of the novel is not chronological.

Prologue
Ram Mohammad Thomas is arrested by the police after winning the quiz show W3B; he is accused of cheating. He is being interviewed and tortured by the police because nobody believes that he really knew the answers to the questions. A female lawyer called Smita comes to his rescue, telling him that she will defend him in court and help him to get the prize money. Thomas starts telling her the story of him winning the show and the story of his life.

1,000 Rupees - The Death of a Hero
Thomas and his friend Salim are in a movie theatre and about to watch a film with Salim's favourite actor, Armaan Ali. The boys are enjoying their free afternoon and the reader finds out more about Salim's craze for Armaan Ali. He has been a fan of this Bollywood movie action hero all his life and hasn't missed a single one of his films. Salim is obsessed with Ali. When the actor's girlfriend leaves him, Salim gets very mad and tries everything to comfort Ali. In between sequences from the movie that they are watching, the reader is informed about a viewer who has taken a seat next to Salim and trying to get into intimate physical contact with him. As it turns out, this man is Armaan Ali, who has disguised himself. Realising that his favourite actor is homosexual, Salim runs home and destroys everything he has collected about him.

1,000 Rupee question and answer
Can you name the blockbusting film in which Armaan Ali starred with Priya Kapoor for the very first time? (44 3)

a) *Fire*, b) *Hero*, c) *Hunger*, or d) *Betrayal*

Answer: d), which Thomas knows due to Salim's obsession with Armaan Ali.

2,000 Rupees - The Burden of a Priest
In this chapter the reader finds out about Thomas' childhood as an orphan, when he was educated and taken care of by the Catholic Church. Thomas is abandoned as a baby on the doorstep of a Catholic sisterhood. They take care of him and place him for adoption but nobody is interested in him for quite some time. After being adopted by a couple, the Thomases, things seem to be looking up, but fate has other things in store for him. His foster mother runs off with another man and his foster father leaves him with Father Timothy, a Catholic priest. Father Timothy cares for him and becomes a father figure for him. He gives him the name(s) Ram Mohammad Thomas, in honour of, and to "satisfy" all the religions in India and, in doing so, tries to ward off religiously based prejudice against Thomas in his life ahead. After a few years with Father Timothy, a new priest arrives, Father John. Father John is a homosexual and drug-addict, who often has visitors at night who share his interests. This causes much tension between the two priests. When a young, adolescent, backpacking tourist arrives, Father John ends up sleeping with the boy, whose name is Ian. Thomas witnesses this incident and tells Father Timothy, who comes to Ian's rescue. In the ensuing raging argument, Father John murders Father Timothy in cold blood, before killing himself too. Afterwards, Ian

reveals to Thomas that he (Ian) is Father Timothy's clandestine (secret) son. Thomas becomes truly an orphan, and is sent to an Orphans' Home. From this point on, Thomas' fate alters for the worse.

2,000 Rupee question and answer
What is the sequence of letters normally inscribed on a cross? (**63** 4)

a) IRNI, b) INRI, c) RINI or d) NIRI

Answer: b), which Thomas knows from a Christian crosses which he saw when living with Father Timothy.

5,000 Rupees
Thomas and Salim live in a big slum in Mumbai. Although only eleven and thirteen years old, they both have full-time jobs and share an apartment, or "chawl" as they are called, which is really no more than a tiny room with walls made of cardboard. It is cramped, dirty and gives no privacy. Not only can people hear everything that is going on in other chawls, they can often see into the next one, because of holes in the "walls".

A family moves in next to them, a couple with a daughter, Gudiya, with whom Thomas falls in love. Mr Shantaram, her father, used to be a professor of astronomy but has lost his job. Now he comes home drunk regularly, beats up his wife and daughter and later sexually abuses his daughter. Due to the thin walls of the buildings in the slum, Thomas and Salim witness everything but have to listen helplessly. One evening Mr Shantaram scalds (burns) his daughter's face with a cup of hot tea and when she tells Thomas that she will kill herself to be saved from her father, he swears to protect her. When he wants to teach Mr Shantaram a lesson when he comes home drunk one evening, Mr Shantaram falls down the stairs and dies. Thomas panics and runs away to Delhi, leaving everything and everyone behind.

5,000 Rupee question and answer
Which is the smallest planet in our solar system? (**82** 1)

a) Pluto, b) Mars, c) Neptune or d) Mercury

Answer: a), which Thomas knows because of Mr Shantaram, who used to be an astronomer.

10,000 Rupees – A Thought for the Crippled
Thomas and Salim have first met in a Juvenile Home in Delhi. The living conditions are very bad, the place is overcrowded and the deputy sexually abuses any boy he wants to. Boys from the Juvenile Home are sold regularly to a man called Maman, who turns out to be the employer of child beggars. He adopts Salim and Thomas for money from the Juvenile Home and starts to teach them how to be professional beggars. When Thomas and Salim suspect that they are going to be physically harmed – seriously, namely blinded – they run away.

10,000 Rupee question and answer
Surdas, the blind poet, was a devotee of which god? (**112** 10)

a) Ram, b) Krishna, c) Shiva or d) Brahma

Answer: b), which Thomas knows because he and Salim were taught this by Masterji in the Home (**106**). There is also a connection to the threat of blindness, which will have jogged Thomas' memory.

50,000 Rupees – How to speak Australian

Thomas works as a domestic servant for the Australian Defence Attaché, the Taylors. He is only 14 when he works there and witnesses how very badly the Australian family treats their servants. They are shown no respect and treated as second (or third!) class citizens – and that in their own country! Some are fired because of minor offenses; others steal from the family and are fired. Thomas is informed that he will only get his salary when he behaves well. When Thomas finds out that Mr Taylor works as a spy he informs the officials and the Taylor family has to leave India.

50,000 Rupee question and answer

When a government declares a foreign diplomat persona non grata, *what does it mean?* (**137** 19)

a) the diplomat is to be honoured, b) that the diplomat's tenure should be extended, c) that the diplomat is grateful or d) that the diplomat is not acceptable

Answer: d), which Thomas knows because it is what Mr Taylor becomes; the High Commissioner says this (**135** 22)

100,000 Rupees – Hold on to your Buttons

Thomas works as a waiter in a cocktail bar and meets a rich Indian who tells him his life story. He is the owner of a big button making factory and has led a happy life until he met his wife, a black woman who bewitched him and his family. She turned his life into misery. He sent his brother into a mental asylum with her help and took over the company. The price for all this is a life with his now detested wife Julie, who blackmails him now to satisfy all her wishes.

100,000 Rupee question and answer

What is the capital of Papua New Guinea? (**155** 16)

a) Port Louis, b) Port-au-Prince, c) Port Moresby or d) Port Adelaide?

Answer: c), which Thomas works out by a process of elimination (the guy in the bar says he spent his honeymoon in "Port Louis, Mauritius"; Julie comes from Port-au-Prince, Haiti; and Adelaide is in Australia (he knows this from the Taylors)

200,000 Rupees – Murder on the Western Express

Thomas takes the train to Agra, in order to meet Salim again. He has taken all the money he has earned at the Taylors and in his other jobs and hidden it in his underwear. He shares the compartment with an Indian family and a young mother. He makes friends with the family's son and tells him where he has hidden the money, not long before they are robbed. The robber molests the women and Thomas manages to kill him with his own weapon. He loses all his money.

200,000 Rupee question and answer

Who invented the revolver? (**173** 19)

a) Samuel Colt, b) Bruce Browning, c) Dan Wesson, or d) James Revolver

Answer: a), which Thomas guesses (he saw the name "Colt" on the gun used in the train hold-up). (**171** 8)

500,000 Rupees – A Soldier's Tale

Thomas and his friends have to hide in a bunker because it is the time of the war between India and Pakistan about the region of Kashmir. There is the danger of bombings and the population is sent into bunkers. Thomas and the other people in the bunker listen to a soldier who has fought in various wars against Pakistan and tells them about the tragedy of war.

500,000 Rupee question and answer
Which is the highest award for gallantry given to the Indian armed forces? (**198** 13)

a) Maha Vir Chakra, b) Param Vir Chakra, c) Shaurya Chakra or d) Ashok Chakra

Answer: b), which comes up in a conversation between Dhyanesh and Balwant, at which Thomas is present (**186**)

1,000,000 – License to Kill

Salim and Thomas meet again in Mumbai and spend some time together. Salim tells him that he has worked for a man who turned out to be a contract killer. In addition, Salim finally managed to get small acting jobs in Bollywood movies. When the contract killer gets the order to kill the producer of Salim's movies, Salim takes the chance not only to save the producer's life but also to take revenge on Maman by having him killed by the contract killer.

1,000,000 Rupee question and answer
…from the world of cricket. How many Test centuries has India's greatest batsman Sachin Malvankar scored? (**216** 1)
a) 34, b) 35, c) 36 or d) 37

Answer: c), which Thomas knows from the description of the cricket match and Ahmed's betting (**212 ff**)

10,000,000 Rupees – Tragedy Queen

Thomas works as a domestic servant in the household of a former Bollywood star, Neelima Kumari. He is treated very well. She even pays for his apartment and pays him a regular wage. Thomas finds out that she is beaten up by her boyfriend brutally. Because her stardom has vanished and she is no longer the Tragedy Queen and heroine but only an aging actress, she endures this abuse. When her mother dies and after a director refuses to offer her a role as a heroine in one of his new movies, she commits suicide.

10,000,000 Rupee question and answer
Neelima Kumari, the Tragedy Queen, won the National Award in which year? (**241** 15)

a) 1984, b) 1988, c) 1986 or d) 1985

Answer: d), which Thomas knows because he lived with her for three years!

100,000,000 Rupees – X Gkrz Opknu (or A Love Story)

Thomas works as a guide at the Taj Mahal. He has got the job by being cunning and because he can speak English. Japanese tourists mistake him for a tourist guide and from then on he earns his money with guided tours. He stays in a room with a boy who has a speaking disorder and enjoys his life with the other tenants, mostly young, single people who work hard to support themselves and their families. He falls in love with the prostitute whom he meets when he accompanies four college students who have booked a tour with him. Nita is forced into prostitution by her brother and Thomas wants to pay off her brother so she is free.

100,000,000 Rupee question and answer
*In which play by Shakespeare do we find the character Costard? (**297** 30)*

a) King Lear, b) The Merchant of Venice, c) Love's Labour's Lost or d) Othello

Answer: c), which Thomas doesn't know, but is helped by Mr Chatterjee via the telephone Lifeboat

1,000,000,000 Rupees – The Thirteenth Question
Thomas is about to win the quiz show but the quiz master interrupts the show before the last question. He wants to bribe Thomas into accepting the money he has won so far, and not answer the last question. Thomas instead threatens to kill the quiz master, because he has found out the he was the boyfriend of Neelima Kumari. He is the one who has beaten her up so badly. The quiz master tells Thomas the correct answer to save his own life and Thomas wins the 1,000,000,000 Rupees.

1,000,000,000 Rupee question and answer
*Beethoven's Piano Sonata No. 29, Opus 106, also known as the 'Hammerklavier Sonata', is in which key? (**305** 9)*

a) B flat major, b) G minor, c) E flat major, or d) C minor

Answer: a), which Thomas is told in the washroom (see above)

Epilogue
Smita fights for Thomas and has got him out of prison. The production company of the quiz show is forced to pay the prize money and goes bankrupt. The quiz master dies two months after the show under mysterious circumstances. Thomas frees the child beggars and puts them in the care of well-known child-welfare agencies. He pays the money for Nita's freedom to her brother and marries her.

II. Module 1: The life of an Indian orphan

2.1 Einführung

Sachanalyse

Indien ist mit über 1 Milliarde Einwohnern eines der bevölkerungsreichsten Länder der Erde. Zugleich gehört es aber auch zu den ärmsten Ländern mit sehr großen sozialen Unterschieden innerhalb der Bevölkerung. Das strenge Kastensystem teilt in Privilegierte und Nicht-Privilegierte ein und das Leben des Einzelnen ist dadurch eingeschränkt und nahezu vorbestimmt. Die Kinder leiden am stärksten darunter. 46% der Kleinkinder in Indien leiden an Unterernährung. 33% der Kinder kommen bereits untergewichtig auf die Welt. Etwa 350 Millionen Menschen leben unterhalb der Armutsgrenze, das sind etwa 27 Prozent der Gesamtbevölkerung. Unter den 15- bis 45-Jährigen sind 33 Prozent aller Frauen und 28 Prozent aller Männer unterernährt. In der Altersgruppe von Kindern bis fünf Jahren liegt die Kindersterblichkeit bei 7%.

Quelle:
Online-Link: 579875-0001

In den ärmsten Regionen Indiens leben viele Waisenkinder – auf Grund der fehlenden sozialen Infrastruktur auf sich alleine gestellt – auf der Straße. Viele dieser hungernden Kinder leben im größten Elend und sind gezwungen zu arbeiten – um leben zu können. An Schule ist nicht zu denken. Auch werden viele Kinder Opfer von Misshandlungen und Gewalttaten. Arme Familien sind in Indien teilweise sogar gezwungen, ihre Kinder zu verkaufen, um überhaupt überleben zu können, oder sie dazu zwingen auf der Straße Geld verdienen, um ihre Familie finanziell zu unterstützen. Skrupellose Gangs verstümmeln sogar systematisch Kinder, damit sie mehr Geld beim Betteln „verdienen" (die Gangs nehmen natürlich das meiste Geld von den Kindern) – siehe Zusatztext: *The Real Slumdog Millionaires* ab Seite 326 in der Lektüre). Sollten Waisenkinder in die Obhut von kirchlichen oder wohltätigen Organisationen gelangen, können sie auf eine weitgehend normale Kindheit hoffen. Viele von ihnen gelangen aber in die Hände von Kriminellen und werden zu Kinderbettlern ausgebildet oder zur Prostitution gezwungen.

Das Leben der Hauptperson des Romans, Ram Mohammad Thomas, ist bestimmt von Unruhe und Unsicherheit. Als Waise wird er zunächst von Nonnen aufgezogen, später von einem englischen Pfarrer und schließlich im Jugendheim. Aus diesem wird er adoptiert, aber nur von einem Verbrecher, der ihn zu einem Kinderbettler macht. Er muss schnell erwachsen werden, sich eine Unterkunft und eine Möglichkeit Geld zu verdienen, suchen. Dies tut er mit niemals nachlassendem Eifer und Zuversicht, dass sich eines Tages alles zum Guten wenden wird. Bei Problemen hat er niemanden, der ihm hilft, er ist immer auf sich allein gestellt. Als Waise und Bewohner eines Slums weiß er, dass er nahezu vogelfrei ist und keinen Schutz von den Behörden oder der Polizei erwarten kann. Sein Leben ist von Kindheit an bestimmt von Ablehnung, Missbrauch und Respektlosigkeit. Obwohl er fleißig und ehrlich ist, wird er entlassen, seine Ersparnisse, die er sich hart erarbeitet hat, werden gestohlen. Doch trotz alledem verliert er nicht den Mut und schöpft seine positive Lebenseinstellung nicht zuletzt aus der Freundschaft mit Salim und der Liebe zu Nita.

II. Module 1: The life of an Indian orphan

Lernziele
- die SuS wenden ihren aktiven Wortschatz zum Thema „Familie" an
- die SuS wenden die Technik der „Clustern" an
- die SuS reflektieren über ihre subjektiven Empfindungen zum Thema „Familie"
- die SuS aktivieren ihr Hintergrundwissen zum Thema „Waisen" in Deutschland und Ländern der 3. Welt
- die SuS wenden die Methode der Bildanalyse an
- die SuS erarbeiten anhand der Kapitel *2,000 Rupees A Burden of a Priest* und *10,000 A thought for the Crippled* der Lektüre exemplarisch das Leben eines Waisen in Indien anhand des Ich-Erzählers
- die SuS analysieren den Text des Kapitels *10,000 Rupees A thought for the Crippled* und lernen das Leben von indischen Waisen als Kinderbettler kennen
- die SuS erarbeiten in Gruppen eine Präsentation zu einer Organisation ihrer Wahl, die sich mit der Unterstützung von Waisen in Indien und der Fürsorge für sie beschäftigen

2.2 The importance of a family

Übersicht der Unterrichtseinheiten

Materialien: Moderationskarten / flash cards Worksheet 1: Orphans Lektüre, Kapitel: *2,000 Rupees: The Burden of a Priest* Worksheet 2: A job for an orphan: child beggar *10,000 Rupees: A Thought for the Crippled*, pp. 83 – 113 DVD Kapitel 4 (siehe auch Module 5)	**Kompetenz:** Leseverstehen, soziale Kompetenz bei PA und GA, emotionale Kompetenz (Empathie, Sich-Hineinversetzen in die Situation der Hauptperson des Romans)	
Ablauf	**Impulse**	**Sozialform Methode**
a) Brainstorming zum Thema Familie mit Hilfe von Moderationskarten	Einstiegsfrage an Tafel / Eröffnungsfrage	TA / EA GA / Diskussion
b) Brainstorming zum Thema Waisen anhand eines Bildes / Fotos	TA *Orphans* Bilder Worksheet 1, Bildanalyse	EA GA / Diskussion
c) Abschlussdiskussion	*Name possible help organisations for orphans in Germany and describe an orphan's life as you'd imagine it.* *Describe an orphan's life in a 3rd world country. Discuss the differences and what they mean for the children's future.* Ergebnissicherung durch Tafelanschrieb entweder als Tabelle oder als Mindmap.	GA / Diskussion TA
d) Worksheet 2: *A "job" for an orphan: child beggar*, Lektüre, *5,000 Rupees A thought for the Crippled*	Arbeitsteiliges Lesen der Lektüre, Ergebnissicherung durch Präsentation	GA TA / Präsentation
e) Abschlussdiskussion der Präsentation		GA / Diskussion

II. Module 1: The life of an Indian orphan

Didaktische Anmerkungen

Das Leben der SuS unterscheidet sich völlig von dem der Hauptperson der Lektüre. Um die Lebenssituation von Ram Mohammad Thomas den SuS näherzubringen, sollen sie zunächst ihre eigene Familiensituation beschreiben und bewerten. Selbst bei Problemen mit Eltern und Geschwistern ist davon auszugehen, dass niemand eine Familie missen möchte. Um diese Phase so frei wie möglich zu gestalten, wird mit Moderationskarten gearbeitet, auf denen die SuS mit einem Stichwort die an der Tafel befindlichen Fragen beantworten sollen. Anschließend werden die Moderationskarten nach Themen geordnet („Clustern"). Eine Bewertung und Diskussion der genannten Aspekte sollte sich anschließen.

Aufgaben und Lösungen

1. *Explain what you like / dislike most about your family. Write ONE word for each on the two flashcards given to you and put them on the board.*
2. *Name in one word what you would miss the most about your family if they were gone and write it on the third flashcard and put it on the board.*

Individuelle Lösungen.

WS1 Orphans

Didaktische Anmerkungen

Nachdem die SuS sich mit ihrem persönlichen Familienleben beschäftigt haben, sollen sie sich der Figur des Ram Mohammad Thomas annähern. Ihnen werden nacheinander zwei Bilder von Waisen gezeigt, ein Gemälde aus dem 19. Jahrhundert, auf dem zwei Waisenjungen abgebildet sind und ein Foto eines indischen Waisenmädchens auf einer Mülldeponie. Zunächst wird den SuS nur das erste Bild präsentiert, welches dann beschrieben und interpretiert werden soll. Die SuS sollen ihre Interpretationsansätze anhand des Bildes begründen können, weitgehenden Spekulationen sollte vorgebeugt werden.

Im Anschluss an die Bildanalyse sollen die SuS Angaben dazu machen, welche Möglichkeiten es für Waisen in Deutschland gibt und diese dann denen für Waisen in 3. Welt-Ländern wie Indien gegenüberstellen.

Aufgaben und mögliche Lösungen

Gemälde

1. *Look at the picture (called* Orphans*) and describe it in detail.*
   - two boys in torn clothes, one leaning against the wall, the other one lying in his lap, in front of them a bowl of food, sad looks on their faces, dark colours, white wall as contrast to dark clothes of children
2. *Interpret the picture, taking the following aspects into consideration:*
   - *the painter's intention / the painting's message*
     painter wanted to show orphans' situation by showing them as sad and neglected children who are alone and without any warmth, care or love
   - *how he conveys his intention through the picture*
     the painting's message is conveyed by the choice of colour contrast and the focus on the children. Even though the surroundings are invisible, the viewer is convinced that there isn't anything positive around the children, that they are alone and desperate.
   - *the effect on the viewer*
     the painting leaves the viewer in a sad mood, feeling sorry for the

II. Module 1: The life of an Indian orphan

children on the painting, wondering what could have been done for them
- your personal opinion about how the painter managed to transport his message through the picture
individual answers

Photographie:

1. *Look at this photo of an orphan girl in India and describe it in detail.*
girl in dirty clothes, possibly on a rubbish dump; firm, almost empty look into the camera

2. *!nterpret the picture taking the following aspects into consideration:*
   - *the photographer's intention / the painting's message*
   photographer wanted to show the life of orphans in a third world country, having to work on rubbish dumps to make a living is only an example of how their life might look like
   - *how he conveys his intention through the picture*
   contrast of innocent face and dirty background
   - *the effect on the viewer*
   photograph leaves an impression on the viewer because the girl doesn't seem to be ashamed of what she's doing, she's looking straight into the camera, this normality shall make the viewer think about the living conditions of children in third world countries
   - *your personal opinion about how the photographer managed to transport his message through the photo*
   individual answers

Comparison of orphans' situation in Germany and 3rd world countries:
Germany: parents can name a guardian to take care of their children in the event of an early death of the parents. If there isn't anybody to look after the children they are sent to a foster family, a children's home or a join an assisted living project for adolescents. The most common NGOs to take care of orphans are the SOS-Kinderdörfer, the Deutsches Rotes Kreuz and Christian social service organisations.

There aren't any of these organisations in most third world countries, the children are left alone when they don't have any family to take care of them. There are a few Christian service organisations but places are rare, there are way more orphans than organisations to take care of them. The children are responsible for themselves, even at a very young age and are likely to grow up in poverty. Often children are forced to become criminals or prostitutes to survive.

WS 2a "job" for an orphan: child beggar
Didaktische Anmerkungen
Die SuS können anhand des Kapitels *5,000 Rupees A thought for the crippled* einen Einblick in das Leben von Waisen in Indien erhalten. Der Beruf des Kinderbettlers ist durchaus üblich und wird auch von Nichtwaisen „ausgeübt", die professionelle Organisation liegt jedoch in den Händen von Banden, die ausschließlich mit Waisen arbeiten. Sie beuten die Kinder nicht nur aus, sondern misshandeln sie und bestimmen ihren Tagesablauf, an eine Flucht ist kaum zu denken, weil die Banden, die die Slums unter sich aufgeteilt haben, Flüchtlinge stets zu ihrem Besitzer zurückbringen. Im Buch geraten die Jungen vom Regen in die Traufe, der Leiter des

II. Module 1: The life of an Indian orphan

Jugendheims, in welchem Salim und Thomas untergebracht sind und zu Freunden werden, verkauft sie an Maman, einen Kriminellen, der seinen Lebensunterhalt mit Kinderbettlern verdient. Recht- und schutzlos sind die Jungen ihm ausgeliefert, ihnen gelingt jedoch die Flucht und sie beginnen gemeinsam ein Leben in einem der größten Slums von Mumbai.

Die SuS lesen zunächst das Kapitel *5,000 Rupees* arbeitteilig und bearbeiten die Arbeitsaufträge in drei Gruppen. Für die Präsentation der Ergebnisse sollten Poster und ein Overheadprojektor (oder ein Smartboard) zur Verfügung stehen. Im Anschluss bietet es sich an, die Lektüre mit dem Film zu vergleichen. Ein entsprechendes Worksheet ist unter Modul 5 (WS 23) zu finden.

Die Aufgabenstellung ist zweigeteilt. Zunächst bearbeiten die SuS in Partnerarbeit den Lebenslauf von Thomas und Salim und erstellen ein Organigramm des „Unternehmens" von Maman. Diese Arbeitsschritte sind notwendig für die Bearbeitung der zweiten Hälfte des Arbeitsauftrages, für welchen die Lerngruppe in zwei Teile geteilt wird. Alle SuS erhalten den Arbeitsauftrag, sich die Lebensgeschichten der entstellten Bettlerkinder durchzulesen und sich Notizen zu machen. Dann sollen die SuS zwei unterschiedliche Briefe verfassen. Eine Hälfte der Klasse verfasst einen Brief an die Eltern der Kinder – hier wird davon ausgegangen, dass die Kinder noch Familie haben, in einem kurzen Lehrervortrag müsste darauf hingewiesen werden, dass nicht alles Waisenkinder in Indien wirkliche Waisen waren, sondern auch von ihren Eltern verkauft werden (siehe Sachanalyse). Die andere Hälfte der Lerngruppe schreibt einen Brief an eine Organisation, wie z. B. das Rote Kreuz, welche sich dem Schicksal der Kinder annimmt und für sie sorgen könnte. Hier müssen die SuS einen noch aggressiveren Ton anschlagen, um die Verantwortlichen davon zu überzeugen, dass ausgerechnet sie aus den Händen von Maman befreit werden müssen.

Aufgaben und Lösungen
Work with a partner
1a. *Read the chapter 10,000 Rupees and make curriculum vitae (CVs) for Thomas and Salim.*
1b. *With the help of the CV, write their biographies and describe their characters. What are Thomas and Salim really like?*
2. *Draw an organization chart of Maman's child beggar business.*
Get together in groups. Read the children's biographies Thomas and Saliam are talking to and take notes. Then work on ONE of the following tasks.
3. *Thomas can write. Choose one of the crippled children who told him his story and make Thomas write a letter home to the child's parents asking for help.*
or
4. *Write a letter to a welfare organisation asking for help. Your letter has to be quite "aggressive" if you want to convince them that you out of a million orphans need their help!*
Prepare a poster, PPT presentation or presentation on an overhead projector.
Homework: Clarify what Thomas means by the sentence: "We are both orphans, with no hope of being 'restored'."

1a) Model CV

	Thomas	**Salim**
Personal Information Name: Address(es) House number, street name, postcode, city, country: Telephone: E-mail: Nationality: Date of birth:	*Ram Thomas Mohammad* *Delhi Juvenile Home for Boys, Turkman Gate, India* *Indian* *uncertain, 8 years old*	*Salim* *Delhi Juvenile Home for Boys, Turkman Gate, India* *Indian* *uncertain, 7 years old*
Education and training (school, foreign languages)	*taught English in reading, writing and speaking by Father Thomas*	*none*
Work experience	*none yet*	*none yet*
Additional information / interests:	*interested in surviving and finding friends*	*very interested in Bollywood movies and Indian actors*
Future Plans work in… / as…	*nothing specific*	*becoming a famous Indian actor*

II. Module 1: The life of an Indian orphan

1b) Biography / Characterisation:

Thomas	Salim
- after his stay with Father Thomas he is sent to a Juvenile Home in Delhi (**83** 24) at only 8 years old - terrible living conditions (**83** 25 – **84** 1) - bad conditions for education (**84** 1 – 8) - poor diet, malnutrition (**84** 8 – 13) - sexual (**84** 22) and physical (**84** 21) abuse by deputy, Mr Gupta, nicknamed the Terror of Turkman Gate (**84** 17) - instead of being educated he and the other boys are put in front of the TV (**84** 23 – 28) - low expectations concerning his future (**85** 10) - low self-confidence (**85** 11) - transfer from Father Timothy's house was like a transfer from heaven to hell (**85** 15 – 16) - is grateful for his fate when he hears the other boys' stories (**85** 16 – **86** 7) - he became their leader (**86** 8) because he spoke English - special treatment because of this skill (**86** 13 – 18) - tells Salim his Muslim name because he doesn't want to lose him as a friend (**88** 1) - becomes Gupta's enemy because he rescued Salim from him (**89** 13)	- Salim Ilyasi arrived in very bad conditions (**86** 24) - wheatish complexion, cherubic face, curly black hair and when he smiles his cheeks dimple. - seven years old - keen, questioning mind - comes from a very poor family, father was a labourer, his mother a housewife, his elder brother worked in a tea stall - lived in a village in Bihar, which was predominantly Hindu, but there were a couple of Muslim families too, like Salim's. - attended the village school - in "January", there was a rampage in which Salim's Muslim parents and brother were killed by Hindus. (**87** 3 – 23) - he escaped to Delhi with no food or clothes or a familiar face, he spent a few days delirious with fever and grief in the station, before a constable discovered him and sent him to the Juvenile Home (**87** 24 – 28). - he has bad dreams at night, he has begun to hate and fear all Hindus. (**87** 29 – 32). - almost sexually abused by Gupta (**88** 2 – **89** 7)
Character sketch: Thomas Ram Mohammed is very lonely and lost. Having lost his "father", he is sad and scared. Still, he is not desperate or depressed; he manages to see the good in everything bad. He sees the future positively, finding friends easily and being accepted by most of other people because of his positive, open and friendly nature.	**Character sketch**: Salim is quite naïve, he lives in a fantasy world of Bollywood heroes and heroines. He has lost his complete family in a tragic incident and is lost, sad and confused. Thomas rescues him from sexual abuse but for all his life he is afraid of abuse (**89** 15 – 16) and homosexuals (see Chapter 1 of the novel).

II. Module 1: The life of an Indian orphan

2) Organisational chart

```
┌──────────────┐    ┌─────────────────────────────┐    ┌──────────────┐
│  Punnoose,   │    │   Maman "Uncle"/ Sethji     │    │   Mustafa,   │
│   helper     │    │ Babu Pillai, head of school │    │   helper     │
└──────────────┘    │    for disabled children    │    └──────────────┘
                    └─────────────────────────────┘
```

lure children with false promises (**89** 13–15; **96** 18–22), especially crippled children because they make more money as child beggars (**103** 27 – **104** 15)

give them vocational training to increase income as beggars (**99** 25 – **101** 14)

"motivate" them by putting them under physical and psychological pressure and by punishing them (**99** 19–24) and imprisoning them (**97** 29 – **98** 13)

earning a lot of money by running „school" for crippled and a gang (**101** 28–29; **102** 10–11; **103** 14–26; **107** 11–13)

3) / 4)
(**101** 23 – **105** 21): *students will write individual letters*

Ashok, a thirteen-year-old with a deformed arm, has given up, is grateful for two meals a day.

Raju, a blind ten-year-old, was punished because he didn't earn enough, is often hungry.

Radhey, an eleven-year-old with a leg missing, knows Neelima Kumari, goes to her house when he needs money and food.

Moolay, a thirteen-year-old with an amputated arm, hates his life, but can't run away because of the gang structure in Mumbai; he will always be brought back to Maman.

Sikandar, "imported" from Pakistan, deformed head and face, of great value for Maman because of this deformation.

Letter 1. Homework:

Thomas knows that his and Salim's fates can almost certainly not be changed. They will never live in a happy and "normal" family. Both are lonely and too old to be adopted in a country where there are too many orphans to be rescued. They can only hope to be treated well by the people in whose care they end up, such as Father Thomas and Maman. Their friendship is the only thing that can replace a family.

II. Module 1: The life of an Indian orphan

2.3 Life in the slums

Übersicht der Unterrichtseinheiten

Materialien: Worksheet 3: *Slums* Lektüre, Kapitel: *5,000 Rupees* (**65** 26 – **80** 10)	Kompetenz: Leseverstehen, soziale Kompetenz bei PA und GA, emotionale Kompetenz (Empathie, Sich-Hineinversetzen in die Situation der Hauptperson des Romans)	
Ablauf	**Impulse**	**Sozialform Methode**
a) Brainstorming zum Begriff *Slum*	Describe a slum with appropriate adjectives.	TA
b) WS 3 *Slums*	Look at the photos and discuss whether the adjectives we've collected are appropriate. Name the most important ones.	TA (markieren, hervorheben)
c) Bearbeitung der Arbeitsaufträge des Worksheets, Vergleich der Ergebnisse		EA
d) Abschlussdiskussion	Read **78** 22 – **79** 30.	EA

WS 3 Slums
Didaktische Anmerkungen

Um die SuS auf das Leben in den Slums einzustimmen, werden ihnen zwei Fotos aus Slums präsentiert. Als Vorarbeit sollen die SuS Adjektive zu dem Begriff *slum* an der Tafel sammeln. Danach werden die beiden Fotos (eventuell als Folie) präsentiert und es wird überprüft, ob die genannten Adjektive als Beschreibung passend sind und ob es noch weitere gibt. Im Anschluss sollen die SuS einen Tag im Slum anhand ihrer eigenen Vorstellungen in einem kurzen Text beschreiben und dem Plenum vorstellen. So kann im Anschluss anhand des Kapitels *5,000 Rupees* überprüft werden, ob das tatsächliche Leben im Slum den Vorstellungen der SuS entspricht.

Die Dramatik des Kapitels *5,000 Rupees* wird aufgegriffen, indem die SuS die Technik des „stream of consciousness", die Swarup in dem Kapitel verwendet, erläutern. Die vierte Aufgabe des Worksheets kann entweder im Anschluss an die vorangegangenen Arbeitsaufträge oder als Hausaufgabe bearbeitet werden.

Aufgaben und mögliche Lösungen

1. *Brainstorm on which adjectives best describe a slum and write them in this box:*
   The students are likely to name *dirty, filthy, unhygienic, unhealthy (disease ridden), overcrowded, lacking privacy / cramped, impoverished* and related adjectives.
2., 3. und 4. Individuelle Lösungen
5. *Read the chapter 5,000 Rupees and compare the description of Thomas' and Salim's life in the slum with your description. Find differences and similarities.*
   Siehe Synopse zu diesem Kapitel auf Seite 11 für eine Zusammenfassung der Beschreibung vom Leben im Slum.
6. *Comment on the author's "stream of consciousness" technique* (**78** 22 – **79** 30).

The author uses this technique to heighten the reader's attention and to increase the dramatic aspect of the story. Thomas knows that what he has done is wrong and that he shouldn't have killed Mr Shantaram. The consequence in India is to be sentenced to death. Thomas would have accepted this sentence, even though he only wanted to protect Gudiya from the abuse through her father. The students should identify Thomas' dilemma and give their own opinion about the fatal accident to Mr Shantaram.

2.4 Welfare organisations in India

Übersicht der Unterrichtseinheiten

Materialien: Das Internet! Worksheet 4: *Welfare organisations in India*	Kompetenz: Leseverstehen, soziale Kompetenz bei PA und GA, emotionale Kompetenz, Recherchefähigkeiten, Präsentationskompetenz Methodenkompetenz (Internetrecherche)	
Ablauf	**Impulse**	**Sozialform Methode**
a) Recherche im Internet bezüglich Hilfsorganisation in Indien, die sich vornehmlich um Waisen kümmern	Work out a presentation on a welfare organisation that helps orphans in India.	GA
b) Präsentation		TA / OHP / Smartboard

WS 4: Welfare organisations in India
Didaktische Anmerkungen

Zum Abschluss des Moduls sollen die SuS sich mit den Hilfsorganisationen beschäftigen, die versuchen, das Leben von Waisen in Indien zu verbessern. Die SuS sollen im Internet recherchieren und eine der Organisationen in einer Präsentation vorstellen. Damit dieser Arbeitsauftrag sorgfältig ausgeführt werden kann, sollte mindestens zwei Doppelstunden zur Verfügung stehen. Die Präsentation kann als Powerpointpräsentation oder als Poster erfolgen. Die Ämteraufteilung kann von den SuS selbst vorgenommen werden, es sollte aber darauf geachtet werden, dass jedes Gruppenmitglied eine Aufgabe hat, die er oder sie für eine erfolgreiche Präsentation erfüllen muss.

Besonderer Hinweis an LuL

Für diese Aufgabe gibt es keine vorgefertigte Lösung. Die SuS sollen selbständig im Internet recherchieren und sich die für ihre Präsentation nötigen Informationen selbst erschließen. Die SuS wenden ihre Medienkompetenz an, um die Aufgabe zu bewältigen und finden durch die Recherche im Internet ihre eigenen Lösungen zur Aufgabe (*task-based learning*). Diese Vorgehensweise erfordert ein hohes Maß an Selbständigkeit und Teamfähigkeit; beide Kompetenzen benötigen die SuS in ihrem weiteren Leben. Der Aspekt der Sprachmittlung wird bei dieser Aufgabe ebenfalls berücksichtigt, da die SuS Informationen deutscher Internetseiten zum Thema ins Englisch übersetzen müssen bzw. die Informationen in die Zielsprache übertragen müssen. Dies schult die allgemeine Sprachmittlung und vereinfacht die Orientierung der SuS in einem englischsprachigen Land, da sie durch die Übung zunehmend Techniken erlernen und mit Hilfsmitteln umzugehen lernen.).

Niedersächsisches Kultusministerium, Kerncurriculum für das Gymnasium – gymnasiale Oberstufe, Englisch, S.15

III. Module 2: The lives of the whites in India

3.1 Einführung

In diesem Modul wird die Lektüre mit dem Thema „Kinderarbeit in Indien" verknüpft. Kinderarbeit in Indien ist nicht nur in Steinbrüchen, Webereien oder in der Bekleidungsindustrie noch üblich, sondern 12,6 Millionen Kinder arbeiten nach Angaben der indischen Regierung als Hausangestellte. Dies sind 30,5% der unter 14-jährigen, bei einem Anteil von arbeitenden Kindern im Alter von 5 – 14 Jahren von 14%. Die Ursachen für Kinderarbeit sind vielfältig. Es gibt eine Hohe Zahl von Waisen, für die es keine ausreichende staatliche Fürsorge gibt. Des Weiteren ist Kinderarbeit in Indien in der indischen Gesellschaft traditionell verankert, die Toleranzschwelle ist also sehr hoch, außerdem sind Kinder sind billigere und „unkompliziertere" Arbeitskräfte als Erwachsene. Bisherige Gesetze gegen Kinderarbeit wurden ignoriert oder die Sanktionen hatten keinen ausreichen abschreckenden Charakter. In Indien gibt es kein nationales Gesetz, das ein allgemeines Mindest-Arbeitsalter vorschreibt. Allerdings gibt es eine Auflistung von Beschäftigungen und Prozessen, die Kinder unter 14 Jahren nicht verrichten dürfen, da sie ihre Gesundheit schädigen können. Durch den *Child Labour Act* (1986) wurde zwischen „ungefährlichen" und „gefährlichen" Tätigkeiten unterschieden. Offiziell war es Kindern unter 14 Jahren demnach erlaubt in Haushalten, Garküchen, Straßenläden oder im Verkauf gegen Bezahlung zu arbeiten. Seit 1996 gibt es Strafen für Personen, die Kinder an gefährlichen Arbeitsplätzen beschäftigen. Im Oktober 2006 traten strengere Regeln zu Kinderarbeit in Kraft. Demnach ist nun auch die Beschäftigung von Kindern unter 14 Jahren, in den bisher „ungefährlichen" Tätigkeitsbereichen, wie in Hotels, Garküchen oder in Haushalten offiziell verboten. Die Regelung umfasst auch Rehabilitationsmaßnahmen für die Kinder, sowie Strafen für die Verantwortlichen. Problematisch ist, dass Heimarbeit als privat gilt und gesetzlich daher nicht geregelt ist. Im Januar 2004 startete die indische Regierung ein nationales Kinderarbeitsprojekt in 50 Provinzen, das eine bessere Bildung, vor allem auch für arme und arbeitende Kinder, garantieren soll. Darüber hinaus existieren viele Programme, die von anderen Verwaltungseinheiten, von Bundesstaaten oder Distrikten, getragen werden. Meist werden diese in Zusammenarbeit mit internationalen NGOs (*"non-governmental organisation"*) durchgeführt. Ein bisheriger Erfolg ist, dass in den letzten 10 Jahren der Prozentsatz der eingeschulten Kinder gestiegen ist und sich die Alphabetisierungsraten verbessert haben.

Viele ausländische Arbeitgeber sind sich der Tatsache, dass sie gegen ein Gesetz verstoßen entweder nicht bewusst oder sie ignorieren es, weil sie der Meinung sind, dass sie den Kindern durch den Lohn, den sie ihnen zahlen, helfen oder sie argumentieren, dass die Kinder durch die Beschäftigung, die schließlich leicht zu verrichten ist, berufliche Fähigkeiten erlangen. In den Industrienationen ist Kinderarbeit längst verboten, doch in den Ländern der dritten Welt wird die billige und unproblematische Kinderarbeit gern in Anspruch genommen; Kinder sind weder gewerkschaftlich organisiert noch kennen sie ihre Rechte; zusätzlich gibt es eine hohe Anzahl williger Arbeitskräfte. Die Tatsache, dass im Jahr 2000 die Anzahl der beschulten Kinder und die Alphabetisierungsrate erhöht haben, ist nur ein Schritt in die richtige Richtung, es müssen noch viele weitere folgen.

Quelle:
Online-Link: 579875-0002
Quelle:
Online-Link: 579875-0003

Quelle:
Online-Link: 579875-0004

Quelle:
Online-Link: 579875-0005

Quelle:
Online-Link: 579875-0006

Online-Link: 579875-0007

Lernziele

- die SuS lesen das Kapitel *50,000 Rupees* intensiv und eignen sich Basiswissen zum Leben von indischen Jugendlichen als Hausangestellte / Kinderarbeit in Indien an.
- die SuS erlangen anhand des Textes Kenntnisse über das Verhalten von (einigen) Weißen in Indien gegenüber Einheimischen
- die SuS beurteilen das Verhalten von Einheimischen und nehmen unter diesem Gesichtspunkt zum Inhalt des Kapitels *50,000 Rupees* Stellung
- die SuS erweitern ihr Basiswissen zum Thema Kinderarbeit in Indien anhand eines Sekundärtextes und verknüpfen so die Handlung der Lektüre mit der reellen Situation von jugendlichen Hausangestellten in Indien
- die SuS lernen anhand der Blog-Einträge, die sie online finden, die reelle Situation von jugendlichen Hausangestellten kennen und nehmen Stellung
- die SuS beurteilen die gegenwärtige Situation von jugendlichen Hausangestellten in Indien

3.2 Juvenile domestic servants

Übersicht der Unterrichtseinheiten

Materialien: Lektüre, *Kapitel: 50,000 Rupees How to speak Australian* Worksheet 5		**Kompetenz:** Leseverstehen, soziale Kompetenz bei PA und GA, emotionale Kompetenz (Emphathie, Sich-Hineinversetzen in die Situation der Hauptperson des Romans)
Ablauf	**Impulse**	**Sozialform** **Methode**
a) Brainstorming zum Titel des Kapitels	TA *How to speak Australian*, Eröffnungsfrage	Unterrichtsgespräch
b) Lektüre des Kapitels *50,000 Rupees*	TA Aufgaben zum Text Übergang zum Thema *Child Labour in India* durch Diskussionsfrage	EA Unterrichtsgespräch
c) WS 5: *Child Labour in India*	Arbeitsaufträge Diskussion im Plenum der Antworten der SuS zu den Aufgaben 3. und 4.	EA / PA Unterrichtsgespräch
d) von SuS gefundene Blogs im Internet Abschlussdiskussion	Arbeitsaufträge Präsentation der Ergebnisse als Overhead-Folie *Get back to chapter* (50,000 Rupees) *again.* Give examples of the Taylor's attitude towards the domestic staff. Comment on the way the Taylor's treat their domestic servants. Find other examples of how white foreigners treat their domestic servants in India in the blogosphere.	EA / PA Unterrichtsgespräch

III. Module 2: The lives of the whites in India

Didaktische Anmerkungen

Das Leben von Weißen in Indien wird im Roman in zwei Kapiteln angesprochen. *2,000 Rupees The Burden of a Priest* berichtet von Thomas' Leben bei dem katholischen Priester Father Timothy und das Kapitel *50,000 Rupees How to speak Australian* handelt von Thomas' Zeit als Hausangestellter bei einer australischen Diplomatenfamilie in Mumbai. In diesem Modul wird der Schwerpunkt auf das Kapitel *50,000* gelegt. Der Lektüretext bietet eine Untersuchung des gegenwärtigen Verhältnisses zwischen Weißen und Einheimischen an und lässt sich mit Sekundärtexten verknüpfen. Zunächst werden die SuS sich mit dem Thema Kinderarbeit in Indien befassen. Der Zusammenhang zur Lektüre besteht aufgrund Thomas' Alter. Er ist 14, als er für die australische Familie arbeitet und somit minderjährig. Anschließend werden die SuS mit einem Zeitungsartikel aus dem *Guardian*, in welchem es um das vorgeblich rassistische Verhalten von Australiern gegenüber indischen Studenten geht, sowie einem von SuS ausgewählten Blog-Eintrag, arbeiten. Besonders der Blog-Eintrag muten einer Zeitreise zurück in die Kolonialära an.

Zu Beginn der Arbeit mit dem Kapitel *50,000 Rupees* wird der Titel des Kapitels an die Tafel geschrieben und die SuS sollen Vermutungen über die Handlung des Kapitels äußern. Anschließend lesen die SuS das Kapitel und machen Notizen zum Arbeitsverhältnis zwischen Thomas und den Taylors. Die SuS sollen ihre Notizen dahingehend sortieren, was ihnen ungewöhnlich oder sogar illegal an dem Beschäftigungsverhältnis erscheint. So kann anschließend der Bogen zum Thema Kinderarbeit in Indien geschlagen werden, denn im Lektüretext finden sich Hinweise auf die Illegalität von Thomas' Beschäftigung als Hausangestellter. Nach der Lektürearbeit sollte durch eine offene Frage überprüft werden, wie viel die SuS über das Thema Kinderarbeit in der Dritten Welt bereits wissen, bevor mit der Bearbeitung des Sekundärtextes begonnen wird. Genannte Aspekte können bereits an der Tafel gesammelt und im Anschluss an die Arbeit mit WS5 *Child Labour in India* überprüft werden. Zum Abschluss gehen die SuS zurück zur Lektürearbeit und überprüfen die Einstellung der Taylors zu ihren Angestellten. Sie werden feststellen, dass die Taylors ihre Angestellten keinesfalls gleichwertig behandeln, sondern voller Ablehnung und Vorurteile sind. Nur Thomas wird aufgrund seiner Englischkenntnisse und seines Alters – nämlich als Spielkamerad für die Kinder – akzeptiert. Nachdem sie die Einstellung der Taylors gegenüber den Hausangestellten herausgearbeitet haben, suchen die SuS im Internet nach Blogs, in welchen Weiße, die in Indien leben, sich über ihre Hausangestellten austauschen. Die Ergebnisse dieser Suche sollen thematisiert werden, da sich lebhafte Diskussionen ergeben werden.

Aufgaben

Read the chapter 50,000 Rupees and takes notes about the working relationship between Thomas and the Taylors.
Note things that seem unusual or even illegal to you and give reasons why.

Lösungen

1. – **114, 3** → *Thomas is 14 years old and thus it is illegal to employ him, he is too young.*
   – **114, 12 – 16** → *Servants are "second-class citizens", they are not important for the Taylors, nor for the census, they are "invisible".*

- **114**, 30 – 31 → *racism towards Indians; Mrs. Taylor of the opinion they are all drunks*
- **116**, 19 – 20; **118**, 3 – 11; **119**, 20; **120**; 7 → *Taylors treat Thomas well because he is baptized and speaks English; racism is selective*
- **117**, 21 – 23, **118**, 27 – 30 → *Thomas is a typical child labourer, a domestic servant who only has to do "light" and easy work around the house.*
- **120**, 10 – 15 → *illegal treatment of Thomas as a domestic servant, not paid regularly but family saves wages, which he will only get if he behaves "well"*
- **127**, 25; **128**, 1 → *has to do everything the Taylors ask him to do, here: picking up dog's excrement*
- **136**, 24 – 25; **137**, 1 – 5 → *in the end, Thomas beats them with their own arrogance when he is behind Colonel Taylor's deportation from India*

2.
- Thomas' age (14) is a "problem" as an employee of the Taylors.
- In Germany, children aren't allowed to be employed under 16. Some of the students who have minor jobs might know that Thomas' employment is illegal.
- Thomas doesn't get his wages but is told that the Taylors will give them to him when he quits the job, but only if he behaves well. No employee should have his or her pay made dependant on behaviour and every employee has the right to regular wages on a weekly or monthly basis.
- The Taylors' actions suggest strongly that they know Thomas' employment is illegal. If they employed him properly they would not only have to pay him on a weekly or monthly basis but also let him take part in the census.
- The census man knows that the Taylor's employment of Thomas is illegal but ignores this for a bottle of whisky.

Child Labour in India
Didaktische Anmerkungen

Indien ist ein Land, in dem Kinderarbeit verbreitet und akzeptiert ist. Kinder arbeiten in Webereien, Steinbrüchen und Schmuckfabriken unter menschenverachtenden Umständen. Sie sind unterernährt, haben keine Bildung und wurden nicht selten an den Besitzer der Fabrik oder des Unternehmens verkauft, entweder, weil ihre Familie arm war oder weil Schulden abzubezahlen sind. Dieser Bereich der Kinderarbeit wird in dem vorliegenden Sekundärtext nur am Rande erwähnt, da eine Parallele zur Lektüre gezogen werden soll und somit die Kinderarbeit in Haushalten im Vordergrund stehen muss. Die LuL sollten die SuS jedoch auf das Ausmaß von Kinderarbeit besonders in Indien hinweisen und sie darauf aufmerksam machen, dass große weltweite und (laut stern.de bzw. CBC news) auch deutsche Unternehmen ihre Produkte von Kindern herstellen lassen, wie z. B. GAP, Esprit oder Heine.

Quelle: Online-Links:
579875-0008
579875-0009

Mediationsaufgabe

Als Zusatzaufgabe sollen die SuS im Internet nach einem oder mehreren Blogeintrag- oder einträgen suchen, der oder die einen Eindruck der Einstellung von in Indien lebenden Weißen zu ihren Hausangestellten vermittelt. Schlüssel-worte bei der Internetrecherche sollten *domestic servants, India, working conditions* und beispielsweise *Britons* sein. Sollten die SuS einen deutschen Blog finden, sollte die Verwendung durch LuL gestattet werden, da die Aufgabe der SuS dann die der Mediation sein wird, indem sie beispielsweise eine Zusammenfassung des Textes auf Englisch erstellen sollen. Die Sus präsentieren ihre Ergebnisse im Plenum.

III. Module 2: The lives of the whites in India

Aufgaben (WS 5: Child labour in India):
1. Read the text and summarize it in your own words.
2. Give your opinion about the present state of child labour.
3. Comment on the Taylor's practice of employing Thomas at the age of 14.

Mögliche Lösungen:
1. Child Labour is still a big problem in third world countries such as India. Not only do children have to work in quarries or factories but also as domestic servants. Children as young as ten have to do what is called "light work" in households. Their working conditions are bad and often they are abused physically or sexually. They are placed in their employers' homes by agents who sometimes don't even tell the parents where their children live. Some of the children don't get enough to eat and have to give their wages to their agents. Child labour is a modern kind of slavery which keeps the children going to school and getting a proper education. The Indian government has not yet initialized any laws to prohibit child labour or to punish the employers of children. Since 2004 there has been a minimum age for child labourers by law, a law which still isn't enforced strictly enough.
2. individuelle Lösungen
3. – The students should be able to work out that the Taylors know that they are employing Thomas illegally. Otherwise they wouldn't have bribed the census man and would pay Thomas in the appropriate manner, i.e. with a weekly or monthly salary.
   – By telling him that he will be paid at the end of his employment, they are blackmailing him into staying with them and keeping him from complaining about his working conditions. They know he is an orphan and that there won't be anyone protecting or rescuing him from them.
   – Thomas is clever but not clever enough to notice that he is at the mercy of the Taylors, he feels that they treat him fairly. He hands Colonel Taylor over to the Indian police because he feels the Colonel has done something wrong, not because he wants to get rid of his exploitative employer.

Quelle:
Online-Link: 579875-0012

Um Worksheet 5 als Klausur einsetzbar zu machen, schlagen wir die folgenden Ersatz- bzw. Zusatzaufgaben (hier je mit Lösungen) vor. Das Worksheet ist auch über klett.de online (als editierbares Download) verfügbar.

4. Point out the reasons why child labour in 3rd world countries today is so common.
cheap labour leads to cheap products; very fierce 1st world market competition forces prices down (*Geiz ist geil* etc.); extreme poverty and large families force children into work; lack of laws prohibiting child labour; ignorance of 1st world countries, lack of information about working children and the negative effects on their lives; problem is not "interesting" – welfare organisations don't support working children as much as they could and should

5. Write an open letter to the Indian government asking them to finally pass laws that criminalize child labour.
Individuelle Lösungen. Erwartungshorizont:
Students should refer to the text as a basis for their arguments and give examples of the effects of child labour on children's futures. In order to merit a good mark, there should be at least three arguments to support the students' opinion, and the letter should have a clear structure: an introduction, a main part consisting of three paragraphs supporting the author's arguments and a conclusion.

3.3 Racism against Indians in Australia

Übersicht der Unterrichtseinheiten

Materialien: Lektüre, *Kapitel: 50,000 Rupees How to speak Australian* Worksheets 6-7	**Kompetenz:** Leseverstehen, soziale Kompetenz bei PA und GA, emotionale Kompetenz (Empathie, Sich-Hineinversetzen in die Situation der Hauptperson des Romans)	
Ablauf	**Impulse**	**Sozialform Methode**
a) Brainstorming zum Titel des Worksheets	TA Racist attacks on Indian students in Australia	Unterrichtsgespräch
b) WS6 *Racial attacks in Australia: why only Indians?*	Ergebnissicherung durch Diskussion und TA	EA Unterrichtsgespräch
c) *Worksheet 7 Australia – racist towards Indians?*	Ergebnissicherung durch Diskussion und TA	

Sachanalyse / Didaktische Anmerkungen

2011 wollten immer weniger indische Studenten in Australien studieren. Waren es laut der Einwanderungsbehörde 2008 – 2009 noch 65.503 indische Studenten gewesen, die in Australien studiert haben, waren es 2009 – 2010 nur noch knapp die Hälfte. Australien genoss in Indien keinen guten Ruf. Ein Grund für den Rückgang könnten die vielen Fälle von rassistisch motivierten Übergriffen auf Inder gewesen sein. Ausländische Studenten waren in Australien eigentlich mehr als herzlich willkommen, denn mit ihren Studiengebühren unterstützten sie die Universitäten, die sich ohne sie finanziell gar nicht halten konnten. Allerdings sah man es gar nicht gerne, wenn sie auch noch als Kellner oder Tellerwäscher ihren Lebensunterhalt verdienten und dabei „einem Australier den Arbeitsplatz wegnahmen". Es ist eine Ausrede wenn von Regierungsseite gesagt wurde, dass die damals starke australische Währung oder gar strengere Visa-Bestimmungen am Rückgang indischer Studentenzahlen schuld waren. Denn Studenten aus anderen Ländern wie z. B. China oder Malaysia ließen sich ganz offensichtlich nicht davon abhalten in Australien zu studieren, ihre Anzahl war ungefähr gleich geblieben. Es gab eindeutig ein Problem zwischen Australiern und Indern.

Quelle: Online-Link: 579875-0010

Im Kapitel *50,000 Rupees* wird von Mrs Taylor eine rassistische Äußerung gegenüber Indern getätigt, nämlich, dass sie allesamt Trinker seien (**114**, 30 – 31). Mr Taylor unterstützt die Ansicht seiner Frau und Thomas berichtet, dass die Taylors öfter abwertende Äußerungen über das Trinkverhalten von Indern machen. Zu ihm sind die Taylors nur freundlich, weil er getauft ist und Englisch spricht. Rassistisches Verhalten beinhaltet das Einordnen von Menschen in Klassen und Thomas ist zwar Inder und damit den Taylors untergeordnet, durch seine Bildung wird er von ihnen jedoch aufgewertet und dementsprechend anders behandelt.

Australien wird den SuS als Land bekannt sein, in welchem Rassismus gegen die Aborigines ein Thema war und vielleicht noch ein Thema ist. Dass es in Australien rassistische Übergriffe auf Inder gegeben hat und zwar so zahlreich, dass auch das Ausland aufmerksam geworden ist, dürfte der Mehrheit der SuS nicht bekannt sein.

III. Module 2: The lives of the whites in India

Die SuS bearbeiten zwei Texte, die sich mit der Thematik des Rassismus gegenüber indischen Studenten in verschiedenen australischen Städten befassen. Der erste Text stammt aus einem Journalistenportal in Indien, der zweite stammt aus der *Times of India*. Beide berichten über die Übergriffe auf indische Studenten. Während im ersten direkt Stellung bezogen und Erklärungen gesucht werden, berichtet der zweite Artikel über das Verhalten der australischen Regierung. Beide Artikel sehen in der wachsenden wirtschaftlichen und intellektuellen Macht Indiens den Grund für die Übergriffe. Der erste Text appelliert daran, den Neid auf die erfolgreichen indischen Studenten nicht weiter zu schüren, der zweite hingegen hat die Erklärungs- und Entschuldigungsversuche des australischen Außenministers zum Inhalt, der durch die strafrechtliche Verfolgung der Angreifer nicht unbedingt die Opfer schützen will, sondern die Verbesserung bzw. Wiederherstellung der (wirtschaftlichen) Beziehungen zwischen Indien und Australien im Vordergrund sieht. Die Opfer scheinen der australischen Regierung nicht wichtig, sie fürchtet vielmehr um ihren guten Ruf in Indien. Diesen wieder herzustellen ist wichtig und nur deswegen nimmt die Regierung zu den Übergriffen Stellung.

Die SuS sollen durch diese Aspekte aus den Texten herausarbeiten und erkennen, wie unwichtig der Einzelne für die Regierung ist. Es sollte sich eine Diskussion darüber entfalten, ob wirtschaftlicher Neid ein Grund für Rassismus ist (hier ist ein Vergleich mit der NS-Diktatur durchaus sinnvoll) und wie das Verhalten der australischen Regierung zu beurteilen ist.

Worksheet 6 Racial attacks in Australia: why only Indians?
Aufgaben:
1. *Read the text and sum up the author's reasons for racist attacks on Indian students in Australia.*
2. *Comment on the author's reasons.*

Mögliche Lösungen
1. – *criminal or opportunistic activities (theft)*
   – *India's astounding success in economic fields*
   – *ignorant attitude of Indian police in minor criminal incidents*
2. individuelle Lösungen

Worksheet 7 Australia – racist towards Indians?
Aufgabe:
Read the text and comment on the Australian foreign minister's way of apologising for the attacks.

Mögliche Lösungen
– The Australian foreign minister promises to punish the people that attacked the Indian students; but probably he only behaves this way because India is an economically flourishing country of great economic importance to Australia.
– The high number of Indian students supporting Australian universities with their student fees makes it important to keep positive relations to India. The question is whether the Australian government would have behaved in the same way if the students came from a country of minor economic importance.
– The foreign minister's excuse seems to be rather opportunistic.

III. Module 2: The lives of the whites in India

Abschlussdiskussion:
1. *Get back to chapter 50,000 Rupees again. Give examples of the Taylor's attitude towards the domestic staff.*
2. *Comment on the way the Taylor's treat their domestic servants.*
3. *Find other examples of how white foreigners treat their domestic servants in India in the blogosphere.*

Lösungen:
1. - *thinks they are dishonest and drunkards (**114**, 30 – 31; **136**, 9 – 12)*
   - *fires people when they have done something wrong, even though it wasn't their fault or a minor incident (**116**, 5 – 6; **129**, 21 – 22)*
   - *treats them as inferiors but pays so well the servant don't complain, disrespect them (**115**, 5 – 11, 16 – 19; **120**, 10 – 15; **122**, 20 – 25; **126**, 5 – 8; **127**, 28 – 31)*
   - *differentiate between Thomas and other servants because Thomas speaks English, he is granted some "extras" (**116**, 19 – 20, 23 – 24; **118**, 11, 27 – 29; **119**, 22 – **120**, 7)*
2. *Individuelle Lösungen.*
   The students should note though, that even though the Taylors treat their servants as inferior persons they pay well and take good care of them. They live in servants' quarters and even a servant's family is allowed to stay with them. They are strict when it comes to theft or using the family's belongings for themselves, then the servant is dismissed instantly. They distinguish between Thomas and the other servants. He has to do only light work, as it is allowed by law, even though the laws about child work are still not distinctive, and he is allowed to watch TV and play with the Taylor's children. The fact that they don't pay Thomas his salary on a weekly basis is a bit odd, though. The reason for this might be that this way they want to conceal the fact that they employ a 14-year-old. Even more disturbing is the fact that he only gets the money if he "behaves well"; this indeed is illegal. The servants don't have any proper contracts, they don't have any insurance and they don't have any holidays, that is illegal, too and the Taylor enjoy the advantages of this insecure status because the servants are afraid of losing their job and thus the Taylors can do with them whatever they want. The fact that several servants robbed them explains the Taylor's fear and bad opinion about their servants, still, as educated and modern people, they should be able to distinguish and not talk about all Indians as "bloody Indians".
3. *Individuelle Lösungen.*

IV. Module 3: The dark side of India

4.1 Einführung

Sachanalyse

Indien ist kein sicheres Land, die Formen der Kriminalität sind vielfältig. Das organisierte Verbrechen beinhaltet Drogenhandel, Waffenhandel, Geldwäsche, Erpressung, Auftragsmorde, Betrug und Menschenhandel. Wenngleich diese Verbrechen auch in der westlichen Welt nicht unbekannt sind, steht Indien vor dem großen Problem der Korruption, welches die Verfolgung und korrekte Bestrafung der Verbrechen erschwert. Die Polizei in Indien ist oftmals korrupt und offizielle Statistiken über Kriminalität der Regierung müssen ebenso angezweifelt werden und die korrekte und menschliche Strafverfolgung und Bestrafung der Kriminellen. In Verhören und in Gefängnissen wird verbreitet gefoltert, die Opfer tragen oft bleibende Schäden davon. Die Polizei genießt Narrenfreiheit, nur selten unternimmt die Regierung weder etwas gegen korrupte Polizeibeamte, noch gegen die Folterungen von Beschuldigten. Der 118-seitige Bericht *Broken System: Dysfunction, Abuse and Impunity in the Indian Police* der Organisation *Human Rights Watch* dokumentiert eine ganze Reihe von Menschenrechtsverletzungen durch die Polizei, einschließlich willkürlicher Verhaftung, Folter und außergerichtlicher Hinrichtung. Die Opfer von Verbrechen können sich in den meisten Fällen einer korrekten Strafverfolgung nicht sicher sein, das Engagement der Polizei hängt nicht selten von der Höhe der Bestechungssumme ab. Somit bleibt Indien in Bezug auf sein Rechtssystem insgesamt rückschrittlich, wenngleich es für Touristen ein sicheres Land zu sein scheint, da diese weniger von Gewaltverbrechen als von der Kleinkriminalität betroffen sind. Viele Blogs Indienreisender berichten davon, dass Taschendiebstahl, besonders in der Umgebung von Monumenten wie dem Taj Mahal und in Großstädten, sowie kleine Betrügereien und „über's Ohr gehauen werden" durchaus üblich sind. Dies ist aber sicherlich keine Besonderheit Indiens. Das Auswärtige Amt warnt deutsche Reisende vielmehr vor der Gefahr von Terroranschlägen, außerdem wird empfohlen, dass Frauen nicht allein reisen.

Quelle: www.hrw.org

Lernziele
- die SuS analysieren einen Cartoon zum Thema *police violence*
- die SuS beziehen die Ergebnisse der Cartoonanalyse auf den Epilog der Lektüre
- die SuS erlernen die Methode der Analyse von Statistiken
- die SuS analysieren Statistiken zum Thema *police violence in India* und vertiefen dadurch ihr Wissen
- die SuS vergleichen die sich auf Indien beziehende Statistiken mit Statistiken, die sich auf die deutsche Kriminalitätsrate beziehen
- die SuS erlangen weiteres Wissen über die Korruptheit der indischen Polizei durch die Analyse eines Cartoons und Sachtexten und wenden dies auf ausgewählte Zitate aus der Lektüre an
- die SuS beurteilen die Situation des Rechtssystems in Indien und vergleichen sie mit der in Deutschland

4.2 Police violence in India

Übersicht der Unterrichtseinheiten

Materialien: WS 8 Cartoon und Foto WS 9a Police violence in India WS 9b Analysing statistics Lektüre *Prologue; 50,000 How to speak Australian*		Kompetenz: allgemeine kommunikative Kompetenzen	
Ablauf	**Impuls**		**Sozialform Methode**
a) WS 8 Police Violence b) WS 9a und 9b: Police Violence in India/ Analysing statistics c) Slumdog Millionaire (85 23; **108** 21 und **237** 16)	Bildimpuls durch Cartoon (stummer Impuls), Interpretation eines Cartoon, anschließend Interpretation eines Fotos Statistiken zur Polizeigewalt in Indien und Methodenblatt *Analysis of Statistics* Sicherung durch Graphik Zitate aus der Lektüre, die sich auf das Thema *police violence in India* beziehen werden den SuS per OHP/Smartboard präsentiert und die SuS bewerten diese.		OHP/Smartboard, UG PA OHP/Smartboard, UG UG

Sachanalyse

Die Polizei in Indien ist nicht nur in Einzelfällen korrupt und unterliegt einer sehr nachlässigen Kontrolle durch den Staat. Nur so ist zu erklären, dass jährlich sowohl über 100 Todesfälle zu verzeichnen sind, die sich in einem Polizeirevier während eines Verhörs ereignet haben. Die Würdigung der Menschenrechte scheint von der finanziellen Situation der Beschuldigten und auch der Opfer abhängig zu sein. Die Polizeigewalt ist bei Demonstrationen ungezügelt und wird strafrechtlich nicht verfolgt.

Quelle: www.survivalinternational.de

Didaktische Anmerkungen

Zu Beginn des Themas analysieren die SuS einen Cartoon zum Thema Polizeigewalt. Zunächst wird der Cartoon beschrieben und anschließend analysiert und von den SuS bewertet. Die SuS sollen erkennen, dass es sich bei den Cartoons um eine Kritik an Polizeigewalt in Europa und den USA handelt. Zum Themenbereich Indien wird mit einem Foto übergeleitet, das den SuS auf OHP oder dem Smartboard präsentiert wird. Die SuS sollen das Foto ebenso interpretieren und mit dem Cartoon vergleichen. Sie sollen erkennen, dass im Unterschied zu den Cartoons die Gewalt der Polizei gegen Zivilisten üblich ist und strafrechtlich nicht verfolgt wird. Bei Zeitreserve kann auf den Fall des entführten Bankierssohn Jakob Metzler hingewiesen werden, in welchem der verantwortliche Kommissar von dem Entführer der Folter beschuldigt und welcher zu einer Geldstrafe verurteilt wurde, hingewiesen werden, um den SuS zu verdeutlichen, dass Polizeigewalt und Folter in Deutschland strafrechtlich verfolgt werden. Der verantwortliche Kommissar hatte dem Entführer des Kindes Schmerzen angedroht, weil er hoffte, das Kind noch lebend vorzufinden und der Entführer das Versteck seines Opfers nicht preisgeben wollte.

Die SuS arbeiten weiter mit zwei Tabellen der National Human Rights Commission, die sich mit der Zahl von Toten sowohl nach Polizeiverhören als auch in

Gefängnissen beschäftigen. Sie interpretieren diese mit Hilfe eines Methodenblattes und wandeln die Darstellungsform der Tabelle in eine Grafik um, die sie dem Plenum präsentieren. Zum Abschluss dieses Abschnittes werden den SuS Zitate aus der Lektüre präsentiert, die sie auf den Begriff der *police violence* hin beurteilen sollen.

WS 8 Police violence

Aufgaben:
1. Look at the cartoon and describe it in detail.
2. Summarise the cartoonist's message. Explain how he uses symbols and words to transport this message.
3. Comment on the cartoon and on the way it criticizes the problem of police violence.
4. Look at the picture and think of a title for it.

Mögliche Lösungen:
1. Police questioning, suspect is threatened by the policemen. The questioning seems to have come to a halt and thus the policemen try to intimidate the suspect with physical pain.
2. The cartoonist criticizes the fact that the police still use torture during interrogation and that this cannot be controlled. It happens in face-to-face interviews when there aren't any other witnesses or when the two policemen leading the interview cooperate and cover for each other. The cartoonist uses symbols such as lamps that are pointing directly towards the suspect and desks that can be found in police stations. The policemen stand above the suspects in a threatening way. The witnesses look helpless and are at the mercy of the policemen, who feel superior to the suspect, they are on the law's side and nobody can prove that they have done anything wrong (because they have a partner to cover for them or can blame the puppet).
3. Individuelle Lösungen.

The cartoon deals with police violence in Western countries. Police violence is prohibited by law and will be prosecuted; still nobody knows what's going on behind closed doors and how high the percentage of violent incidents during police questionings is.
4. Individuelle Lösungen.

WS 9a Police Violence in India und WS 9b Analysing statistics
Aufgaben:
1. Look at the statistics.
2. Interpret them with the help of WS 9b Analysing statistics.
3. Make a graph or several graphs that you think best conveys the message or messages of the grids.
4. Sum up the meaning of each graph in one sentence.

Lösungen
2. The grids show the development of the percentage of deaths in judicial and police *custody in India. The numbers from 2000 – 2001 are the base and the percentage is calculated on this base.*

In the first grid there are two significant increases: in 2005–2006 and in 2007–2008. The reasons for these peaks are unknown and the students should be kept from speculating.

The increase of 44.09% in the second grid in 2002/2003 is based on the number of 127 from the years 2000/2001. The tables show the average increase of deaths in judicial and police custody. There are two peaks in 2002/2003 and in 2007/2008 compared to the base (police custody). The reasons for these peaks are unknown. The reasons are not important, the importance of the grid is the significance of the high number of deaths of people who are in the government's care, even if they are only under the care of the law enforcement authorities.

3. Individuelle Lösungen.
4. Individuelle Lösungen.

Slumdog Millionaire – police violence in India, quotes from the novel

> *I came to fear the police. They were the ones responsible for sending most of the boys to the Juvenile Home.* (**85**, 23 – 24)

> *'How about going to the police?' 'Are you out of your mind? Haven't you learnt anything since Delhi? Whatever you do, wherever you go, never go to the police. Ever.'* (**108**, 21 – 24)

> *I gaze at Neelima Kumari's dead body and I do not know what to do. The only thing I am certain of is that I will not go to the police. They are quite capable of pinning the blame on me and arresting me for murder.* (**237**, 16 – 19)

Aufgaben:
1. Explain the meaning of each quote.
2. Comment on each quote's message and how it supports the accusation that the police in India cannot be trusted.

Mögliche Lösungen
1. Each quote shows that Thomas, being a "slumdog", has learnt not to trust the police because they will not help him. He cannot provide the financial "aid" that is necessary when you seek the police's help in a country like India. The epilogue of the novel proves him right, the police don't believe that he knew the answers to the questions and thus torture him cruelly.
2. The author of the novel makes quite clear that as a member of the lowest caste you cannot hope for the police's help. The numbers of the National Human Rights Commission show that police questionings and jail sentences can even be fatal. Members of the lowest caste and "slumdogs" have to take care of and help themselves without the help of the authorities.

4.3 Crime in India

Übersicht der Unterrichtseinheiten

Materialien: WS 10: India – crime rates Die Lektüre WS 11 Crime in India and Germany		Kompetenz: allgemeine kommunikative Kompetenzen	
Ablauf	Impuls		Sozialform Methode
a) *WS 10: India – crime rates (map)* b) Lektüre: *Epilogue 5,000 Rupees; 10,000 Rupees; 50,000 Rupees; 200,000 Rupees; 1,000,000 Rupees; 100,000,000 Rupees* c) *WS 11 Crime in India and Germany*	Bildimpuls auf OHP/Smartboard Arbeitsauftrag: *Get together in groups and read the chapter of the novel you were assigned. Take notes about the crimes that are described in the text. Be ready to present your findings to the class.* Arbeitsaufträge, Arbeit mit Grafiken, Umwandeln von Daten in eine Grafik		OHP/Smartboard UG GA/UG PA/OHG UG

Sachanalyse

Zuverlässige Quellen für Statistiken über die Kriminalitätsrate in Indien sind schwierig zu finden. Wie schon erwähnt, ist nicht nur die Polizei, sondern auch die Regierung korrupt und es liegt im öffentlichen Interesse, die Zahlen für die Außenwelt zu beschönigen. Verbrechen geschehen in Indien genau wie in jedem anderen Land, wenngleich in Indien eine nicht zu unterschätzende Prozentzahl an Verbrechen zu verzeichnen ist, die gegen die Menschenwürde gerichtet sind, nämlich Menschenhandel, Kinderheirat und die von der Gesellschaft akzeptierte Misshandlung von Frauen und Mädchen. Wie schon erwähnt, rät das Auswärtige Amt alleinreisenden Frauen in Indien zur Vorsicht. In diesem Abschnitt des Moduls wird es um die Verbrechen gehen, die in der Lektüre beschrieben werden und die in den Statistiken wiederzufinden sind.

Didaktische Anmerkungen

Die SuS werden auf das Thema mit einer Karte Indiens eingestimmt, die die Verteilung von Verbrechen landesweit zeigt. Die SuS sollen die Karte beschreiben und im Anschluss die Zahlen und die Aussagekraft der Karte beurteilen. Die LuL müssen die SuS darauf hinweisen, dass es sich bei der Karte nicht unbedingt um eine von der indischen Regierung veröffentlichte Studie handelt. Auf der im Anhang befindlichen Karte von Indien kann von den SuS überprüft werden, um welche Provinzen es sich handelt und von welchen Zahlen der Grafik die Hauptperson des Romans betroffen war (Maharashtra: above 150,000).

Im Anschluss wenden sie sich der Lektüre zu mit dem Auftrag, eine Liste der Verbrechen anzufertigen, die in ausgewählten Kapiteln beschrieben werden. Diese Liste ist nötig, um sie mit der Verbrechensstatistik zu vergleichen. Hier ist anzumerken, dass es sich um eine andere Provinz handelt, die Provinz Arunachal Pradesh weist aber die gleiche Kriminalitätsrate auf wie die Provinz Maharashtra

IV. Module 3: The dark side of India

und ein Vergleich ist somit vertretbar. Die SuS werden in Gruppen aufgeteilt und lesen die Lektüre arbeitsteilig, damit diese Phase nicht zu viel Zeit in Anspruch nimmt. Die Notizen jeder Gruppe sollten dem Plenum kurz vorgestellt werden, damit die Gesamtheit der Lerngruppe einen Überblick erhält.

Zum Abschluss dieser Phase vergleichen die SuS in Partnerarbeit die Kriminalitätsstatiken von Indien und Deutschland. Da die beiden Quellen unterschiedlich dargestellt sind – die von Indien als Tabelle und die von Deutschland als Tortendiagramm – sollen die SuS die Indien betreffende Statistik zunächst in ein Tortendiagramm umwandeln. Dies kann handschriftlich und auf einer OHP-Folie geschehen. Nachdem beide Quellen die gleiche Form haben, sollen die SuS die Kriminalitätsraten miteinander vergleichen und die Unterschiede beurteilen.

WS 10 India – Crime figures
Aufgaben:
Describe what is shown on the map.

Mögliche Lösungen:
The map shows crime figures in the year 2009, in India, by provinces. The key shows that different colours represent different ranges of crime figures. It is significant that areas with big cities show the highest number of crimes and rural areas the lowest. It can be said though that the majority of the Indian subcontinent has a high crime rate. The message of the graph is – in stark contrast to other numbers made available by the government – that India is a dangerous country.

Lösungen zur Lektürearbeit: *Crimes that are described in the novel:*
- **Epilogue**: *police torture, corruption (TV company has bribed police commissioner to have Thomas arrested)*
- **5,000 Rupees: A Brother's Promise**: *child abuse, abuse of women (Mr. Shantaram beating up his wife and daughter and sexually molesting his daughter.*
- **10,000 Rupees: A Thought for the Crippled**: *exploitation of child beggars, corruption of warden of juvenile homes, abuse of children physically, mentally and sexually*
- **50,000 Rupees: How to speak Australian**: *exploitation of under-aged children as domestic workers, theft, physical abuse of servants (even though they have stolen it is illegal to beat them up), police corruption*
- **200,000 Rupees: Murder on the Western Express**: *armed robbery on a train, killing of robber in self-defence, police investigation stops quickly because nobody tells the officials what has happened*
- **1,000,000 Rupees: Licence to Kill**: *contract killer, kills people for money, illegal betting on horses*
- **100,000,000 Rupees: X Gkrz Opknu (or A Love Story)**: *corruption of the police, corruption of doctors (won't help ill boy without being paid for it even though the boy will die), prostitution*

IV. Module 3: The dark side of India

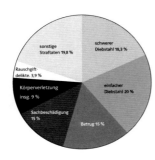

WS 11 Crime in India and Germany

Aufgaben:

1. *Work with a partner. Turn the numbers of the grid (Arunchal Pradesh) into a pie chart.*
2. *Look at the second pie chart about the crime statistics in Germany and compare it with the Indian statistics.*
3. *Find reasons for similarities and differences.*
4. *Relate the graph of the Indian figures to the contents of the novel.*

Lösungen:

2. Both pie charts show that burglary, theft and robbery are the most common crimes. In India criminal assault has the second highest number while in Germany "sonstige Straftaten", meaning traffic offenses and other minor offenses and criminal assault are relatively few. While in India there is a distinction between crimes against women there isn't in Germany. Drug offenses are relatively low in both countries; in India, drug dealers are sentenced to life, while in Germany they are sentenced to long prison terms, and this might be a reason for the low number. Concerning crimes against women and rape in India there certainly is a high number of unreported cases, the same goes for "Sexualdelikte" in Germany.

3. As we have seen in the novel, the problem of poverty leaves theft as the only chance of survival for many people. Women and men steal to take care of their families or simply to survive. Organized robbery is common, thieves sell the stolen goods on to survive or to support their families. The gap between rich and poor makes this problem worse, as well, as does the caste system, which doesn't allow a rise in social standing. Once poor, always poor, the only chance to improve the situation is by stealing. In Germany stealing is done for financial reasons, people don't steal to survive but to resell things. Only expensive goods are stolen, only for resale, not to buy food. In Germany, stealing isn't as "necessary" as in India, here we have a welfare state to take care of the poor.

4. The statistics concerning India correlate with the text of the novel. The author often writes about people having to steal to survive or to support their families, e.g. Lajwanti, who can only pay for her sister's dowry by stealing. The Taylors' servants see wealth and are tempted to steal, knowing they could sell goods on and increase their wages. As far as unreported cases are concerned, the chapter A Brother's Promise supports this assumption; Gudyia doesn't report her father to the police but tells the doctors in the hospital that she had an accident.

4.4 Corruption in India

Übersicht der Unterrichtseinheiten

Materialien: WS 12 Corruption – a cartoon WS 13 India among the most corrupt nations WS 14 Corruption in India – A rotten state		Kompetenz: allgemeine kommunikative Kompetenzen	
Ablauf	**Impuls**		**Sozialform / Methode**
a) WS 12: Cartoonanalyse b) WS 13: India among the most corrupt nations c) WS 14: A rotten state	Bildimpuls durch Cartoon (stummer Impuls) Arbeitsaufträge, Sicherung auf OHP oder Smartboard Arbeitsaufträge, Sicherung im Unterrichtsgespräch Impuls als Folie Abschlussdiskussion zum Thema Crime in India		OHP, UG PA, OHP / Smartboard EA, UG OHP / Smartboard UG

Sachanalyse

2011 war Indien Spitzenreiter unter den korruptesten Ländern Asiens. Übertroffen wurde es nur noch von den Philippinen, Indonesien und Kambodscha. Der Anti-Korruptionsminister war vor kurzem wegen Bestechlichkeit entlassen worden. Laut einem Bericht von Januar 2010 (http://news.oneindia.in/2011/01/31/thousandsprotest-government-corruption-inindia-aid0127.html) begann die Öffentlichkeit sich zu wehren. Demonstrationen gegen Bestechlichkeit fanden statt und die Regierung bemühte sich z. B. im Bereich von Baugenehmigungen durch Ausschreibungen der hohen Bestechungsrate entgegen zu wirken. Im Bereich der Polizei und Regierungsbeamten Bestechungsgelder ließ sich allerdings ein allzu lukratives Nebeneinkommen darstellen. In Indien waren Reiche immer noch gleicher als Arme, wenngleich die Situation sich langsam zu bessern schien.

Didaktische Anmerkungen

Zum Abschluss dieses Moduls beschäftigen die SuS sich mit der Korruption in Indien. Begonnen wird mit der Analyse eines Cartoons, der sich auf die bestechliche indische Polizei bezieht. Im Anschluss sollen die SuS aus Zahlen in einem Sachtext in Partnerarbeit eine Grafik erstellen und diese im Plenum diskutieren. Erweitert werden ihre Kenntnisse über die Gründe für die hohe Rate on Bestechlichkeit in Indien durch einen Sachtext, der sich auch mit der Bekämpfung der Bestechungsrate durch die indische Bevölkerung und die indische Regierung bezieht. Zum Abschluss wird zunächst die Bestechungsrate Deutschlands mit der Indiens verglichen und die unterschiedlichen Rechtssysteme werden beurteilt. Hier sollen mögliche Gründe dafür gefunden werden, warum in armen Ländern die Bestechungsraten immer noch wesentlich höher sind als in Europa und Nordamerika. Eine Worksheet mit Zitaten aus der Lektüre rundet das Modul ab, die SuS sollen erkennen, das Thomas, der immer von der Korruptheit der Polizei betroffen war, sich diese als reicher Mann zunutze macht, wenn auch zu noblen Zwecken.

WS 12 Corruption in India – Cartoon

Aufgaben:
1. Look at the cartoon and describe it in detail.
2. Find a headline for the cartoon.
3. Comment on the cartoon's message.

Lösungen:
1. A motorbike driver is stopped by the police. The sign in the background indicates that the man on the motorbike is wanting to go to Bangalore, a big city in India. The policeman seems to be asking for a certain amount of money from the man to enter the city, which is not allowed. The dog next to him looks yet friendly but is maybe being used by the policeman as a threat. When the man answers that he doesn't have any cash on him the policeman replies that he takes credit cards.
2. Individuelle Lösungen. The fact that a fine to enter a city is illegal should be present in the headline, though.
3. The cartoon illustrates the situation of the corrupt police in India. Due to low wages policemen are open for bribes, a fact which is exaggerated in this cartoon because the policeman seems to have invented a bribe or fine for entering the city of Bangalore. The fact that the policeman says he takes credit cards shows how deeply rooted in Indian society the problem of corruption is. While cash can be hidden and corruption camouflaged, credit card payments can be tracked down and this shows the acceptance of corruption in India not only by the public but also by the government because the police clearly need have no fear of being caught.

WS 13 India among the most corrupt nations

Aufgaben:
1. Read the text and turn the numbers mentioned into a bar chart.
2. Comment on the numbers in your chart, giving possible reasons for the high rates of corruption in Asian countries.

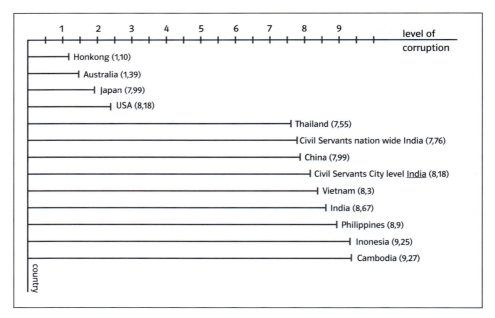

Mögliche Lösungen
1. Bar chart: siehe Diagramm
2. *Poverty and the big gap between rich and poor are the most likely reasons for the high rate of corruption in many Asian countries. Even though most of the countries are democracies and/or republics, the governments are corrupt and sometimes reign like dictators and not prime ministers or presidents. People with money can buy influence and political decisions, leaving the ordinary citizens at their mercy.*

WS 14 Corruption in India – A rotten state
Aufgaben:
1. Read the text and give reasons for the high rate of corruption in India according to the text.
2. Explain how India is trying to fight corruption and comment on these efforts.

Mögliche Lösungen
1.
   - *theft of money by officials; corrupt sale of 2G telecoms licences*
   - *vast growth of infrastructure in India, many possibilities for graft to get lucrative building contracts*
   - *Although India is still growing economically, the stock-market is performing badly.*
   - *high rate of corrupt politicians because companies offer tempting amounts of money for deals*
2.
   - *anti-corruption bodies are emerging, e.g. checking public offers online*
   - *police increasingly arresting and interviewing corrupt politicians*
   - *transparency: showing the public how expensive graft is and how much more could be done with money if there wasn't any graft*
   - *ID scheme for welfare payments to make sure people in need get money*
   - *state has to sell corrupt state-owned companies and cut red-tape*
4. *Individual answers. The student should note though that the efforts of the Indian government are insufficient. They might work in big cities and in big companies with access to the internet and with young employers who want to change something and who are aware of the fact that corruption must be stopped. In rural areas and smaller towns corruption will still be the only way to operate for civilians and businessmen. At present, the wages of government officials are too low and the poverty rate is too high to finally wipe out corruption in India.*

V. Module 4: The media in India: Bollywood movies and international TV

5.1 Einführung

Sachanalyse

Mit der Quizsendung *Who Wants to Be a Millionaire?* beginnt dieses Modul. In einer kurzen Sequenz wird auf die Quizsendung eingegangen, um die SuS auf das Thema einzustimmen und eine Beziehung zur Lektüre herzustellen. Im zweiten Teil des Moduls wird den SuS der Einfluss der Medien auf die Bevölkerung und die besondere Rolle der indischen Filmindustrie des Bollywood-Movies vermittelt. Dieser Abschnitt kann zu einem späteren Zeitpunkt in der Unterrichtsreihe behandelt werden, da es sich anbietet, dieses Modul nach *Who Wants to Be a Millionaire?* zu unterbrechen und mit Modul 1 fortzufahren, um der Handlung der Lektüre zu folgen.

Who Wants to Be a Millionaire? wurde 1998 erstmalig vom englischen Fernsehsender ITV ausgestrahlt. Die Sendung schauten zu den Spitzenzeiten weltweit Millionen von Zuschauern gebannt zu, wenn die typische Musik erklang und sich die Lichter auf den Moderator und den Kandidaten herabsenkten. Die Zuschauer rieten mit und viele haben sich selbst bei der Sendung als Kandidat beworben. In über 100 Ländern der Welt wurde eine Version der Quizsendung ausgestrahlt, in einigen wurde die Sendung nach kurzer Zeit aber wieder eingestellt.

Quelle: de.wikipedia.org

Das Genre des Bollywood Films ist in Deutschland mittlerweile bekannt, deutsche Fernsehsender strahlen regelmäßig Bollywood-Filme aus, es gibt regelmäßige Bollywood-Parties in verschiedenen deutschen Großstädten und die dazugehörigen Accessoires können in Geschäften, die sich ausschließlich dem Thema Bollywood widmen, erworben werden. Auch die Verfilmung von *Slumdog Millionaire* endet mit einer typischen Bollywood-Sequenz, nämlich einer Massentanzszene. Bollywood-Filme sind im höchsten Maße erfolgreich, keine andere Filmindustrie produziert so viele Filme wie die in Indien. Es sind keine großen und aufwändigen Filmproduktionen, sondern es ist vielmehr eine Massenproduktion für die unzähligen kleinen Kinos in Indien. Die Darsteller dieser Filme haben keine Fans, sie haben VerehrerInnen. Man spricht über sie auch als Helden und Heldinnen und die Figuren handeln immer nach einem gleichen Schema, so wie auch die Filme nach einem gleichen und unverwechselbaren Schema aufgebaut sind. Für Westeuropäer muten die Bollywood-Filme seltsam an. Viel Weichzeichner wird verwendet, die Helden sind sowohl verwegene Kämpfer für Recht und Ordnung als auch leidenschaftliche Liebhaber und pflichtbewusste Söhne. Die Heldinnen sind unglaublich schön und haben eine große erotische Ausstrahlung. Damit widersprechen sie dem gängigen Frauenbild in Indien, der Mutter von mehreren Kindern, die sich um den Haushalt und die Familie kümmert und die stets sittsam einen Sari und einen Schleier trägt, um jegliche überflüssige erotische Ausstrahlung zu vermeiden.

Der Roman ist in die Quizshow eingebettet und auch das Thema Bollywood ist mit der Romanhandlung verwoben. So ist Salim ein großer Fan von Armaan Ali, einem großen – fiktiven – Star des Bollywood-Films und Thomas hat bei einer alternden Heldin des Bollywood-Films bis zu deren Freitod gearbeitet. Eine Bearbeitung des

Romans unter dem Obergriff *The media in India* bietet sich nicht nur an, sondern erscheint notwendig.

Lernziele
- Die SuS wenden ihren aktiven Wortschatz bei der Beschreibung eines Fotos an
- Die SuS aktivieren ihr Hintergrundwissen zur Quizshow *Who Wants to Be a Millionaire?*
- Die SuS erkennen den Einfluss von Medien und können diesen beurteilen
- Die SuS lernen das Genre des Bollywood-Movies kennen und können dieses Genre und seine Wirkung auf die Bevölkerung Indiens beurteilen
- Die SuS lernen die Besonderheit der indischen *heroes* und *heroines* in Bollywood-Filmen kennen
- Die SuS beschäftigen sich mit den im Roman genannten Bollywood-Stars Armaan Ali und Nelima Kumari und erarbeiten den Charakter dieser Figuren anhand des Lektüretextes
- Die SuS beurteilen die Rolle der indischen Frau in der Gesellschaft
- Die SuS beurteilen den Erfolg von Bollywood-Filmen und die Diskrepanz zwischen Film und Realität
- Die SuS reflektieren die Unterschiede und Gemeinsamkeiten zwischen der indischen und europäischen Medienwelt und beurteilen diese

5.2 Who Wants to Be a Millionaire?

Übersicht der Unterrichtseinheiten

Materialien: Foto auf OHP-Folie WS 15	**Kompetenz:** funktionale kommunikative Kompetenzen	
Ablauf	**Impulse**	**Sozialform Methode**
a) Präsentation eines Fotos der Sendung *Who Wants to Be a Millionaire?* (eventuell auf OHP) Flashcards, Tafel b) kurzes Partnerinterview	stummer Impuls What do you know about the quiz show Who Wants to Be a Millionaire? Interview als Sprechanlass *Work with a partner and interview each other about the question whether you'd like to be a candidate in a quiz show and what you'd do with the prize money.*	OHP, TA, UG TA PA / UG

Didaktische Anmerkungen
Den SuS wird ein Szenenfoto aus der Fernsehsendung *Who Wants to Be a Millionaire?* als stummer Impuls präsentiert. Die Beiträge der SuS werden in Clustern geordnet an die Tafel gebracht. Im Anschluss erhalten die SuS den Arbeitsauftrag, sich mit einem Partner darüber zu unterhalten, ob er / sie an der Quizshow teilnehmen würde, warum und was mit einem eventuellen Gewinn erwerben würde. Die Sicherungsphase ist somit frei zu gestalten, die Antworten der SuS sollten jedoch auf Flashcards gesammelt werden, um sie zum Ende der Arbeit mit der Lektüre noch einmal vergleichen und Thomas' Verwendung des Gewinnes einordnen zu können.

5.3 The genre of Bollywood movies

Übersicht der Unterrichtseinheiten

Materialien: Filmposter auf Folie bzw. OHP Lektüre Kap. *1,000 Rupees* und *10,000,000 Rupees*		Kompetenz: funktionale kommunikative Kompetenzen	
Ablauf	**Impulse**		**Sozialform Methode**
a) Brainstorming zum Begriff Bollywood b) Farbfolie	stummer Impuls durch Präsentation des Posters eines Bollywood-Films auf OHP Infotext Bollywood-Film, Sicherung durch TA		OHP, TA, UG EA, UG EA, UG

Auf der Seite www.imdb.com können solche Poster gratis und legal heruntergeladen werden.

Didaktische Anmerkungen

Die SuS beschäftigen sich mit dem Genre des Bollywood Filmes. Begonnen wird mit der Präsentation eines Bollywood-Filmposters, welches die SuS beschreiben sollen. Falls sie nicht selbständig auf Unterschiede zu Postern von Hollywood-Filmes eingehen, sollten die LuL mit einem Impuls darauf hinweisen, denkbar wäre z. B. die Präsentation eines Hollywood-Film Posters zum direkten Vergleich. Bei ausreichender Zeit für die Unterrichtseinheit können Trailer zu Bollywood-Filmen angesehen und analysiert werden. Anschließend wird den SuS ein Sachtext ausgehändigt, der die typischen Charakteristika eines Bollywood-Filmes benennt. Die SuS sollen diese herausarbeiten und im Anschluss mit Hilfe ihres neuen Wissens den Bollywood-Film im Allgemeinen mit dem Hollywood-Film im Allgemeinen vergleichen. Sicherlich gibt es SuS, die Bollywood-Filme kennen. Dieses Wissen und die persönliche Meinung dieser SuS sollten für die Abschlussdiskussion für ein Gespräch über das Genre Bollywood genutzt werden.

Aufgaben:

1. *Read the text and take notes about the characteristics of a Bollywood movie.*
2. *Name differences to Western (Hollywood or European productions) movies.*

Mögliche Lösungen:

1. – *Bollywood movies are always musicals: actors have to sing and dance at least once*
   – *when actors can't sing there are playback singers who even have their own fans*
   – *plot is melodramatic with a lot of romance*
   – *luxurious movie equipment, great architecture, beautiful natural surroundings*
   – *love story is complicated due to problems within the lovers' families*
   – *other obstacles such as villains who are against the love affair*
   – *fate makes things turn out well at the end; there always is a happy ending*
2. – *plots of Hollywood/European movies vary more, there can be love stories, thrillers, horror movies, spy movies, etc. Bollywood **always** has a love story*
   – *Hollywood/European movies are mostly not musicals, singing/dancing rare*
   – *sex scenes/affectionate kissing: almost always in Hollywood/European movies*
   – *no religious aspects necessary for a Hollywood/European movie*
   – *there is no pattern for Hollywood movies, they are completely different from each other*

- *Hollywood / European are more successful worldwide because they address a broader audience than Bollywood movies, more money is made in the Hollywood film industry than in the Bollywood film industry though the number of tickets sold for Bollywood films is higher*
- *Hollywood / European movies are produced for big movie theatres and their production takes a longer time, there is no mass production*

5.4 The heroes and heroines of Bollywood movies

Übersicht der Unterrichtseinheiten

Materialien: Fotos auf WS 17 Lektüre: *1,000 Rupees* und *10,000,000 Rupees*	**Kompetenz:** funktionale kommunikative Kompetenzen	
Ablauf	Impulse	Sozialform Methode
a) Brainstorming zu Hauptdarstellern in Bollywood-Filmen	Describe a typical Bollywood hero / heroine	UG
b) WS 17: Lektüre *1,000 Rupees* und *10,000,000 Rupees Tragedy Queen*	Arbeitsteiliges Lesen der Lektüre Arbeitsaufträge	EA; GA; EA und UG

Sachanalyse

Die Diskrepanz zwischen der Scheinwelt des Bollywood-Filmes und der Realität ist der zentrale Aspekt dieses Modulteils. Die Hauptdarsteller in Bollywood-Filme werden aufgrund ihres Lebenswandels und ihrer Rollen in Filmen verehrt. Sie stellen nicht nur Helden dar, sie sind Helden und Heldinnen. Diese Rollen haben bestimmte festgelegte Merkmale, wie z. B. in Bezug auf die männlichen Filmrollen, eine stark maskuline Ausrichtung. Nichts Weiches oder Sanftmütiges darf der Held eines Bollywood-Filmes an sich haben, er muss hart und stark sein. Homosexualität ist weitestgehend immer noch ein Tabuthema in Indien. Homosexuelle werden zwar nicht strafrechtlich verfolgt, aber gesellschaftlich nicht akzeptiert. Männer müssen männlich sein, erst recht, wenn sie Helden in Bollywood-Filmen spielen. Somit bedeutete die Offenlegung einer gesellschaftlich nicht akzeptierten sexuellen Orientierung das Karriere-Aus für Armaan Ali, den Bollywood-Helden der Lektüre.

Ähnliches gilt für die Rolle der Frau in Bollywood-Filmen. Zwar wird sie als sanftmütig dargestellt, aber in anderen Aspekten entspricht sie keinesfalls den traditionellen Vorstellungen der indischen Frau. Heldinnen der Bollywood-Filme sind häufig Kurtisanen, die außereheliche sexuelle Beziehungen haben und ein freies Leben führen. In einem Land, in welchem die Frau laut der hinduistischen Schriften dem Mann Untertan sein soll, ist dies im richtigen Leben undenkbar. Die im Buch dargestellte Bollywood-Schauspielerin Neelima Kumari war ein großer Star des indischen Kinos und hat nun, nach der Beendigung ihrer Karriere, Anpassungsschwierigkeiten, da sie sich nicht in die typische Rolle der indischen Frau in der Gesellschaft außerhalb von Bollywood einordnen kann.

V. Module 4: The media in India: Bollywood movies and international TV

Didaktische Anmerkungen

Die SuS beschäftigen sich mit den Charakteren der typischen Bollywood-Darsteller, des *hero* und der *heroine*, den Hauptdarstellern jedes Bollywood-Filmes. Zunächst werden ihnen Fotos von in Indien bekannten Schauspielern auf einem Arbeitsblatt (WS 17) präsentiert und sie sollen diese in einer kurzen Einstiegsphase analysieren. Die SuS sollen erkennen, dass die Promotion-Fotos der Schauspieler einen bestimmten Zweck erfüllen. Die LuL müssen die SuS darauf hinweisen, dass diese Fotos immer gleich aussehen bzw. immer die gleiche fotographische Machart haben. Die SuS sollen sich nach dieser Einstimmungsphase mit der Darstellung von Bollywood-Schauspielern in der Lektüre befassen. Das Kapitel *1,000 Rupees: Death of a Hero*, in welchem es um den fiktiven Schauspieler Armaan Ali geht, und das Kapitel *10,000,000 Rupees: Tragedy Queen*, das Kapitel über die ebenfalls fiktive Schauspielerin Neelima Kumari, sollen SuS arbeitsteilig lesen. Sie sollen aus dem Lektüretext die Darstellung der Charaktere der beiden Schauspieler herausarbeiten und in eine Graphik übertragen. Im anschließenden Abschnitt werden diese Arbeitsergebnisse dann dem Rollenbild von Mann und Frau in Indien gegenüber gestellt.

Aufgabe (Ws 17):

1. Fill in the grid.

Mögliche Lösungen

1.

A Bollywood Hero	**A Bollywood heroine**
First impression:	**First impression:**
individual answers	*individual answers*
purpose / aim of photographer:	**purpose / aim of photographer:**
show actor in the best possible way to promote him as a hero and star of the Bollywood movie scene – masculine, wild, seductive, attractive	*show actress in the best possible way to promote him as a hero and star of the Bollywood movie scene – beautiful but not erotic, weak, soft, caring, warmhearted*
personal opinion about photo:	**personal opinion about photo:**
individual answers	*individual answers*

2. Get together in groups. Read the chapter 1,000 Rupees: Death of a Hero **or** 10,000,000 Rupees: Tragedy Queen.
3. Describe the character of either Armaan Ali **or** Neelima Kumari based on the text of the novel and fill in the grid with your findings.
4. Taking the fact into consideration that both Ali's and Kumar's careers have ended (Ali's due to his homosexuality and Kumar's because of her suicide), write an obituary for him or her.

3. Armaan Ali

- star: *the ultimate action hero. The Indian Greek god. The heartthrob of millions* (**29**, 12 – 14)
- masculine: *Armaan in a leather jacket. Armaan on a motorbike. Armaan with his shirt off, baring his hairy chest. Armaan with a gun. Armaan on a horse. Armaan in a pool surrounded by a bevy of beauties* (**29**, 18 – 21)
- attractiveness: *Armaan's biceps, he can see the whites of Armaan's hazel-green eyes, the fine stubble on Armaan's cleft chin, the little black mole on Armaan's chiselled nose* (**30**, 9 – 11)
- reluctant to his fans: *Armaan heard the cry, stopped in his tracks and turned around. His eyes made contact with Salim's. He gave a faint smile, an imperceptible nod of acknowledgement and continued walking into the lobby* (**32**, 10 – 13)
- typical Bollywood heroes, fulfilling all the necessary patterns of this film genre: *Armaan plays a gangster in this movie. A gangster with a heart. … Armaan and his mother are climbing towards the shrine of Vaishno Devi* (**35**, 1 – 2) /
Armaan has come to Switzerland, ostensibly to locate a contact, but actually to romance Priya and sing a song, in which he is joined by twenty white female dancers wearing traditional costumes that are rather skimpy for a cold mountainous country (**36**, 13 – 19) /
His vest is soaked in blood. There are bullet wounds all over his body. … He grips her hand. His chest convulses. (**39**, 22 – **40**, 12)
- heterosexual relationship for the public: *Armaan is completely heartbroken. That he has stopped eating and drinking. That he might be suicidal* (**33**, 18 – 19),
- sexual tension in the movie: **36**, 20 – **37**, 5
- hero: *Armaan will kill hundreds of bad guys in revenge, expose corrupt politicians and police officers, and finally die a hero's death* (**35**, 31; **36**, 1 – 2)
- homosexual: *The old man sitting next to Salim shifts uncomfortably in his seat, crossing his legs. I am not sure, but think his hand is massaging his crotch* (**37**, 11 – 13; **39**, 3 – 20) /
I see that the bearded man's left hand has moved on. It is now placed in Salim's lap and rests there gently. … But in that split second Salim and I have seen a flash of hazel-green eyes. A chiselled nose. A cleft chin. (**40**,19 – **41**, 21)
- would lose many of his fans if he was gay, his career would end (**37**, 21 – **39**,2) /
- *As the credits begin to roll over the screen, Salim is left holding in his hand a mass of tangled grey hair … He is weeping. Armaan Ali, his hero, has died* (**41**, 15 – 21) /
'And do you realize the significance of what you have just recounted to me?' 'What?' 'That if this incident was made public, it could destroy Armaan Ali, end his film career. Of course, that will happen only if what you just told me is true. (**41**, 26 – 31)

Neelima Kumari

- <u>obsessed with herself</u>: *Neelima's bedroom is the best room in the flat. .... Next to the dresser is a twenty-nine-inch Sony TV, a VCR and the latest VCD player* (**218**, 25 – 30) /
Glass shelves line the walls, loaded with trophies and awards of all kinds. There is another glass case full of old film magazines. All of them have Neelima Kumari on the cover (**219**, 1 – 3) /
She only buys cosmetics or clothes (**219**, 31 – **220**, 1) /
Come, let me show you something.' She takes me to her bedroom and opens a metal almirah. ...' 'So, Madam, was that the greatest role you ever played?' She sighs. 'It was a good role, no doubt, with a lot of potential for emotion, but I feel that I have yet to play the greatest role of my life.'(**222,** 1 – 30) /
There is excitement in the flat. ... Then I notice that Neelima is crying.(**223**, 10 – 16, 30 – 32) /
I also wonder about her obsession with beauty. Physical beauty. ... Films may end, but the show must go on.' I wonder whether she said this from her heart, or just recited some lines from a film. (**224**, 25 – **225**, 1 – 15)

- <u>still thinks she's a great actress / star</u>: *In her time, she must have been the most famous actress in India* (**219**, 5 – 6) /
'Excuse me, are you Neelima Kumari, the actress?' asks one of them. '...Come, let's have an ice cream,' she says (**220**, 10 – 31) /
Did you see the review of that new film Relationship of the Heart in the Times of India? ... I am getting the review framed.' (**221**, 21 – 29) /
you are too young to know that Neelima Kumari is called the Tragedy Queen of India. (**221**, 32 – 32) /
'Madam,' I ask with concern, 'what happened? Why are you crying?' ... I could summon tears to my eyes at will.' (**224**, 1 – 10)

- <u>expert in the genre of Bollywood film</u>: *From time to time, Neelima teaches me about the art of filmmaking. ... Then she teaches me about genres. 'I hate the movies they make these days, in which they try to cram everything – tragedy, comedy, action and melodrama. No* (**221**, 1 – 21)

- <u>lonely, because she spent her life in the Bollywood film world</u>: *The more I see of Neelima, the more I begin to understand why she is called the Tragedy Queen. ... This man had come to rob her and just because he has seen a few of her films she feeds him biscuits and tea.* (**229**, 10-12) /
'Nothing, Ram. I slipped from my bed and hurt myself. Nothing to worry about.' I know she is lying. That man I saw leaving the flat has done this to her. And in return she has given him cigarettes, whisky and also money. I feel pained and angry, and powerless to protect her. (**230**, 13 – 18) /
There is a man in my life. Sometimes I think he loves me. Sometimes I think he hates me. He tortures me slowly, bit by bit.' (**230**, 30 – 31)

- <u>cannot accept that the days of her stardom are over</u>: *'Well, pardon my saying so, but I heard that part of the reason you quit was because you were not being offered any roles.' Anger flares up on her face. ... I escort the bewildered journalist to the door.* (**232**,6 – 25) /
I want to leave behind an image of unspoilt youth and beauty, of everlasting grace and charm. I don't want to die when I am ninety. How I wish at times I could stop all the clocks of this world, shatter every mirror, and freeze my youthful face in time.' (**233**, 16 – 20) /

A famous producer is coming to the house. Neelima is very excited. She believes he will offer her a role and she will get to face the camera once again. She spends the entire day applying make-up and trying on various outfits. (**233**, 27 – 30)
... is a great role for you, Neelimaji,' the producer is saying. 'I have always been one of your greatest fans. I saw Woman fifteen times. ... She is lucky I didn't cast her as the grandmother. Huh!' (**243**, 1 – 25)/
Finally, she enters her bedroom and inserts into the VCR the cassette of her film Mumtaz Mahal. ... It says, 'National Award for Best Actress. Awarded to Ms Neelima Kumari for her role in Mumtaz Mahal, 1985.' (**237**, 3 – 13)

4. Individuelle Lösungen.
Both actors have led successful professional lives as real Bollywood stars. Armaan Ali and his girlfriend Urvashi were both popular and in the headlines of almost every yellow-pages-magazine. Their break-up was a tragedy for all of their friends, who, like Salim, were devastated. Ali's career is endangered by his homosexuality because this sexual preference doesn't suit a Bollywood hero who has to be tough, masculine, heroic and – maybe most importantly – a womanizer. Not only his fans would abandon him but certainly the Bollywood film industry.

Neelima Kumaria was a great star of the Bollywood scene but for the high price of being lonely after her career. She is very self-centred because there isn't anybody else to take care of – besides her mother, who dies – and she is used to being the centre of attention. When she finds out that her stardom has vanished and even watching her films repeatedly doesn't change the situation for the better she commits suicide. She cannot accept the fact that she has aged and that there is a life after Bollywood. She still lives in the Bollywood world and thinks that she still is the Tragedy Queen.

5.5 Indian woman – heroine, prostitute, worker

Übersicht der Unterrichtseinheiten

Materialien: Foto auf OHP-Folie, WS 18; *Lektüre 100,000,000 Rupees*		**Kompetenz:** funktionale kommunikative Kompetenzen	
Ablauf		**Impulse**	**Sozialform Methode**
a) Fotos von hinduistischen Frauen, Vergleich mit dem Foto der Schauspielerin auf WS 17, Diskussion der Unterschiede		Fotos auf OHP / Smartboard *Find and comment on the pictures.* *Describe a day in the life of an Indian woman as you'd imagine it to be.*	UG, TA UG, TA
b) Lesen der Lektüre c) WS 18, Abgleich mit den Informationen aus dem Sachtext d) Sicherung als TA *Indian Women* e) Abschlussdiskussion		*Comment on the gender roles in Indian society.* *Comment on the success of Bollywood movies taking the difference between real Indian women and the way they are shown in the Bollywood movies into consideration.*	EA UG, TA UG

Sachanalyse

Der letzte Abschnitt des Moduls beschäftigt sich mit der Situation der indischen Frau in der heutigen Gesellschaft. Sie ist eine völlig andere als die der Bollywood-Filme. Es gibt keinen Glamour, keine Romanzen und keine Helden, die eine Frau vor dem Bösen retten. Für viele Frauen und Mädchen ist das Leben in Indien nur von einem bestimmt, dem Dienen für und dem Umsorgen der Familie. Geburten von Mädchen werden nicht gefeiert, sondern die Familie wird bemitleidet, denn Mädchen sind teuer, da eine hohe Mitgift im Falle einer Eheschließung gezahlt werden muss. Sie werden nicht zur Schule geschickt, sondern kümmern sich schon früh um die Familie. Sie arbeiten als Tagelöhnerinnen und verdienen nur halb so viel wie Männer. Sie werden von ihren Brüdern zur Prostitution gezwungen und müssen die Mitgift für ihre Schwestern erarbeiten. Ein selbstbestimmtes Leben als Frau in Indien scheint unmöglich zu sein.

Didaktische Anmerkungen

Der große Unterschied des Lebens indischer Frauen zum Leben der westlichen Frauen ist Thema dieses Modulteils und wird anhand von Bildern, der Lektüre und eines Sachtextes erarbeitet. Die SuS äußern anhand einer Reihe von Fotos, die sie im Internet ausgesucht haben, ihre Eindrücke zur Rolle der indischen Frau. Die LuL sollten gleich einen Vergleich zu dem Foto auf WS 17 der Bollywood-Schauspielerin ziehen, denn zum Abschluss des Moduls sollen die SuS sich mit der Frage beschäftigen, warum die Bollywood-Filme in Indien – bzw. Gesamtasien – so erfolgreich sind und auf die Diskrepanz zwischen Film und Realität eingehen, sowohl in Bezug auf Männer als auch Frauen. Die SuS sollen anhand des Lektüretextes und der Sachinformationen erkennen, dass Indien die Recht der Frau immer noch „mit Füßen tritt" und kein so modernes Land ist, wie es gerne in wäre. Weiter können die SuS den Erfolg der Bollywood-Filme am Ende dieses Moduls nachvollziehen, da sie die Möglichkeit darstellen, in eine Traumwelt zu entfliehen und die Realität für eine Weile zu vergessen. Hier müssen die LuL eventuell erneut darauf hinweisen, dass die Bollywood-Filmindustrie von Massenproduktionen geprägt war, die auch ärmeren Zuschauern den Gang ins Kino ermöglichten. Wie oben erwähnt, gibt es im Internet die Möglichkeit, sich Trailer von Bollywood-Filmen anzusehen und den SuS zu präsentieren. Dieser kurze Eindruck reicht meist schon aus, um die Wirkung auf den Zuschauer und den Unterschied zu westlichen Filmproduktionen zu erkennen.

Die Diskussion soll in der Abschlussphase im Mittelpunkt stehen, da die Informationen aus Lektüre und Sachtext den SuS viele Sprechanlässe liefern. Die LuL sollten sich in dieser Phase möglichst zurückziehen; die Form einer Debatte wäre denkbar, in welcher die SuS ihre Positionen und Gegenpositionen formulieren und ein SuS die Moderation der Diskussion übernimmt.

Aufgaben und Lösungen:

1. *Read the text and explain why the dowry system is prohibited by law in India. Read the chapter: 100,000,000 X Gkrz Opknu (or a Love Story) and make notes on the different life situations of women that are described in the text.*

   The dowry system is prohibited because of the dangers involved for brides and their families. These are not only physical dangers such as dowry murders but also the danger of being ruined financially for the rest of their lives due to absurdly high dowry demands. Another reason might be the fact that daughters are not welcome in families because they are too expensive because the family has to pay the dowry when she gets married. The status of women has to be improved in India and the prohibition of the dowry system is one way to start.

2. Read the chapter: 100,000,000 Rupees and make notes on the different life situations of women that are described in the text.

Lajwanti:
- Unmarried young woman, who has to work for her sister's dowry; so desperate because of the high demands of the husband that she finally steals from her landlady and is arrested, family expects her to do so. Even though she is older than her sister, she has to marry off her sister first because their parents are dead. Only if her sister is married can she look for her own husband. She looks for a husband for her sister in newspapers, her sister doesn't even know her future husband yet (**258**, 30 – **260**, 14; **273**, 13 – **274**, 6; **276**, 31 – **278**, 14; **279**, 18 – **281**, 24)

Rani / Swapna Dewi:
- Widow of a rich man who lives in a big mansion in Agra. Because she doesn't have any children, she rents out the extra rooms in the outhouse to young and poor people. The accommodations are simple and affordable. The fact that she is a widow who is not only still alive but also runs a business and is also friends with the police commissioner and the magistrate, shows that she is either a modern woman or has bought her influence with her inheritance. There is the rumour that Shankar, the boy who cannot speak, is her son because Shankar doesn't have to pay any rent and gets money from his "mother". When Thomas tells her that her son is very ill and needs money, she refuses to help him. She is afraid that her influential and rich friends will find out that she has an illegitimate son – Shankar was born after she had lost her husband and never remarried. (**253**, 24 – **254**, 18; **285**, 1 – **286**, 19)

Nita:
- Young girl who works as a common prostitute because it is a tradition in her background that one girl earns money for the rest of the family while the men benefit from her. Her brother is her pimp and he treats her like his possession and not like a human being at all. When she's badly beaten up by a customer he takes her to hospital, but only so that she can continue working and making money for him. The only way for her to be rescued is Thomas buying her off from her family. (**264**, 15 – **266**, 11; **269**, 11 – **271**, 3; **278**, 15 – **279**, 17; **290**, 6 – **291**, 17; **293**, 23 – **294**, 12)

3. Comment on the situation of women in India today and how this is portrayed in the novel. Find pictures of ordinary Indian women on the Internet to help you.

The text and the novel demonstrate women's problems in various areas of Indian life: married women having to provide for their spouses and work for them either as day labourers or even as prostitutes to pay for the dowry, single mothers and lonely former Bollywood starlets. Smita seems to be the exception, being a successful and independent lawyer. While the other women are dominated by men and rules made my men – Nita by her brother, Rani and Lajwanti by male dominated society and Neelima Kumari because she lets her boyfriend beat her up terribly, Smita seems to be free and able to live a self-determined life, maybe through the death of her father.

Quelle:
Online-Link: 579875-0013

Um Worksheet 18 als Klausur einsetzbar zu machen, schlagen wir die folgenden Ersatz- bzw. Zusatzaufgabe (hier mit Lösungen) vor. Das Worksheet ist auch über klett.de online (als editierbares Download) verfügbar.

4. Explain why the fact that girls are of less value than boys in India might be dangerous for the country's future. If possible, refer to information about other Asian countries.
   - pregnant women might seek an abortion if they find out that they are expecting a girl to prevent high costs for the girl's dowry
   - after the birth of a girl, destitute women kill the baby (this really happens!) to save their family from high financial costs
   - too few females in a society leads to a simple logistical problem: no women = reduced birth rate

Abschlussdiskussion
Individuelle Lösungen.
Gender roles in Indian society are still traditional. Independent women such as Smita are the exception; as the text has shown, even rich women such as Rani have to hide inappropriate details such as an illegitimate child from the public. The women are still dominated by males who dominate society. Men have to be masculine, that's why homosexuality is not accepted in India. While Western movie stars have comparatively few problems with homosexuality, this would be a tragedy for the fans of Bollywood heroes. As the info sheet about Bollywood movies said, the romance between a hero and a heroine are the essence of each movie and a romance can only happen between a heterosexual male and a woman. Again, India fails to play its new, modern role well enough to be fully "accepted".

Bollywood movies are a way for many poor Indians to flee from reality. Gender roles are shown in a romantic way. Men are portrayed as strong but they are also allowed to be soft and to treat their women – both lovers and mothers – respectfully and to enjoy life. They die a happy death because they have fulfilled their duties. The same goes for the women, they like Bollywood movies because their lives are shown in a happy way. They are allowed to fall in love with the man they choose and to enjoy a happy relationship without any obstacles such as caste and insurmountable family problems. Bollywood, like Hollywood, is a dream world but the difference between Bollywood movies and reality is much bigger.

VI. Module 5: The Movie

6.1 Einführung

Sachanalyse
Es ist nicht anzunehmen, dass die meisten SuS den Film *Slumdog Millionaire* kennen. Hier ist nicht die Analyse des gesamten Films, sondern von zwei Filmsequenzen vorgesehen, des Anfangs und der Szenen mit den Kinderbettlern.

Der Film hat nahezu nichts mit der Handlung des Buches gemeinsam, außer der Tatsache, dass ein Junge aus den Slums die Quizshow *Who Wants to Win a Billion?* (WaB) gewinnt. Der Hauptdarsteller heißt Jamal Malik, Salim ist sein Bruder und nicht sein Freund, und Smita heißt Latika. Die Kinder kommen alle aus dem Slum und schlagen sich nachdem ihre Eltern von Hindus umgebracht wurden, gemeinsam durchs Leben. Gemeinsam gelangen sie zu den Kinderbettlern, wo sie eine relativ friedliche Zeit verbringen. Bei der Flucht Jamals vor einer Blendung trennen sich ihre Wege. Jamal und Salim verbringen ihr weiteres Leben als Verkäufer in Zügen und später als Fremdenführer im Taj Mahal. Als sie dort vertrieben werden, kehren sie nach Mumbai zurück und suchen und finden Latika im Rotlichtviertel. Salim erschießt ihren Zuhälter Maman, denjenigen, der alle drei zu Kinderbettlern gemacht hat. Jamal und Salim entzweien sich und während Jamal ein Chai-Wallah wird und ein ehrliches Leben führt, wird Salims und Latikas Leben vom Verbrechen dominiert. Die Handlung des Films ist in das Polizeiverhör eingebettet, der Kommissar übernimmt die Rolle Smitas und schaut sich gemeinsam mit Jamal die Sendung an, um Hinweise für einen Betrug Jamals zu erkennen. Im Verlauf des Verhörs nähern sich der Kommissar und Jamal an, da der Kommissar erkennen muss, dass Jamal kein dummer *slumdog* ist, sondern seine besondere Lebenserfahrung ihn dazu befähigt hat, die Quizshow zu gewinnen. Der Film endet damit, dass Jamal und seine große Liebe Latika ihr weiteres Leben gemeinsam führen werden, was mit einer für einen Bollywoodfilm typischen Tanzeinlage gefeiert wird.

Didaktische Anmerkungen
Durch die Tatsache, dass der Film sich kaum an die Vorlage des Buches hält, können Film und Buch nicht direkt miteinander verglichen, sondern nur Szenen exemplarisch behandelt werden. Hier wird eine Modellanalyse der ersten Szene, dem Verhör, mit dem Prolog, und der Flucht aus dem Lager der Kinderbettler und dem Kapitel *10,000 Rupees* erarbeitet. Mit den Arbeitsblattvorlagen können bei einer zeitlichen Reserve auch noch andere Szenen analysiert werden.

Lernziele
- die SuS eignen sich wichtige Begriffe der Filmanalyse an
- die SuS achten zunehmend auf die einzelnen Elemente, aus denen der filmische Gesamteindruck entsteht
- die SuS reflektieren über ihre bisher eher subjektiven Filmeindrücke und erkennen die manipulative Wirkung filmischer Gestaltungsmittel

VI. Module 5: The Movie

- die SuS reaktivieren ihr Wissen über die Handlung des Romans und ihr Hintergrundwissen, um mit Hilfe des Lektüretextes eine kurze Spielszene zu entwerfen und vorzuspielen
- bei der Erarbeitung der Spielszene wenden die SuS themenspezifisches Vokabular an, das sie durch die Lektüre des Romans erlernt haben
- die SuS wenden ihre Kenntnisse zum Entwurf einer Spielszene an
- die SuS beurteilen die Umsetzung des Romantextes in zwei Szenen des Filmes *Slumdog Millionaire*

6.2 Tools for film analysis

Übersicht der Unterrichtseinheiten

Materialien: WS 19, 20 und 21	**Kompetenz:** Leseverstehen, soziale Kompetenz bei PA und GA	
Ablauf	**Impulse**	**Sozialform Methode**
a) Brainstorming zur Filmanalyse	Einstiegsfrage	Unterrichtsgespräch
b) WS 19		EA
c) WS 20		
d) WS 21		EA

Didaktische Anmerkungen

Es kann nicht davon ausgegangen werden, dass alle SuS Erfahrungen mit der Verwendung von Filmsprache und dem Einsatz von filmischen Mitteln haben. Dies wird vor der eigentlichen Beschäftigung mit dem Film mit wenigen Worksheets (19 – 21) geübt. Falls erwünscht ist, diesen Übungsabschnitt zu vertiefen und auszuweiten, finden sich weitere empfehlenswerte Worksheets in den folgenden Klett Titeln:

- *African Americans in Film*, von Susanne Heinz, Kopiervorlagen 6 bis 10 c (auf Seiten 97 bis einschl. 105 (Module II, *Tools for Film Analysis*, Seiten 15 – 17); Klett 2010, ISBN 978-3-12-577468-1
- *Modern India in Film*, von Monika Plümer, vor allem Kopiervorlagen S1.1 bis S1.7 (auf Seiten 146 bis einschl. 152); Klett 2010, ISBN 978-3-12-577472-8
- *Filmanalyse*, Herausgeber: Thomas Tepe; Klett 2004, ISBN 978-3-12-577463-6

Lösungen

Individuelle Lösungen, dann Austeilen von WS 21 zum Abgleich.

6.3 *Slumdog Millionaire*, Chapter 1: The interrogation

Übersicht der Unterrichtseinheiten

Materialien: Lektüre DVD: **Kapitel 1** bis 4:15'	**Kompetenz:** Funktionale kommunikative Kompetenzen (Hör- und Sehverstehen) Leseverstehen (Lektüretext und Film) Anwendung des aktiven Wortschatzes in Erarbeitungs-, Präsentations- und Diskussionsphasen	
Ablauf	**Impulse**	**Sozialform Methode**
a) Vorbereitung der Spielszenen	Erarbeitung einer kurzen Spielszene anhand Zeilen 1 – 5, S. 11 (Prologue)	GA
b) Presentation der Spielszenen	Präsentation der Szenen, Feedback durch das Publikum	GA
c) Ansehen der 1. Szene des Films (ca. 5 Min.) mit WS 22	Gemeinsames Ansehen der 1. Szene des Films	EA, LV
d) Abschlussdiskussion	Aufforderung an SuS Gemeinsamkeiten und Unterschiede zwischen Film und eigenen Szenen festzustellen und diese zu beurteilen.	Unterrichtsgespräch

The interrogation: Didaktische Anmerkungen

Da die SuS im vorangegangenen Abschnitt in Einzelarbeit und mit Worksheets gearbeitet haben, wird zur methodischen Auflockerung nun von den SuS eine kurze Spielszene in Gruppen erarbeitet und dem Plenum vorgestellt.

Die SuS gehen zunächst zurück an den Anfang der Lektüre und erarbeiten anhand der ersten fünf Zeilen des *Prologue* die Darstellung des Textes. Die Erarbeitung erfolgt in Gruppen und die Zuweisung von Ämtern (*dictionary warden, time keeper*, etc.) ist sinnvoll, damit alle Mitglieder der Gruppe gleichsam an der Arbeit beteiligt sind. Die SuS sollen selbst entscheiden, wer die Aufgabe der Darstellung übernimmt. Für die Erarbeitung sollte den SuS ausreichend Zeit zur Verfügung gestellt werden, um Fehler und Unsicherheiten zu vermeiden. Die Szenen werden dem Plenum vorgestellt und von diesem beurteilt. Die genannten Aspekte, sowohl positiv als auch negativ, sollten für alle erkennbar an der Tafel festgehalten werden, damit sie für den nun folgenden Vergleich mit der Filmszene zur Verfügung stehen.

Aufgaben und Lösungen

1. Read the first five lines of the novel.
   I have been arrested. For winning a quiz show. They came for me late last night, when even the stray dogs had gone off to sleep. They broke open my door, handcuffed me and marched me off to the waiting jeep with a flashing red light. (**11** 1 – 5)
2. Get together in groups of four and prepare a short play / scene which captures the action of these lines. Take notes about the dialogue and practice the scene once you have finished. It should not be longer than five minutes.
1. Individuelle Lösungen.

VI. Module 5: The Movie

Mögliche Lösungen zu Worksheet 22

1. **Brief description of sequence**
   Jamal Malik is interviewed by the police because he won WaB.

   What happens at the level of plot or narration in this sequence?
   scenes from the quiz show and Jamal's everyday life interrupt the interview

   What role does this sequence play within the whole plot of the film (e.g. rising action, climax, turning point, exposition, character development, motifs, patterns, etc.)?
   The main character and his "problem", the fact that he as an unskilled Chai Wallah won the quiz show, are introduced.

   Cinematography: Note composition, camera movement, off-screen space, colour etc.
   The scenes of the police interrogation interact with sequences from the quiz show, e.g. Jamal thinks about the quiz show when he is dipped into a bucket of water brutally by the police officer.

   Note how camera angles, lighting, music, narration, and / or editing contribute to creating an atmosphere in this film.
   The action is lit in the complementary colours yellow (the interview) and blue (the quiz show) to show the dramatic difference between the two situations. The camera alternates between close-ups of Jamal and either the police officer or the talk show host and medium shots of the interview room and the studio. The constant changes of the camera movements and angles create tension and restlessness, and make the viewer want to keep watching.

   Does the scene appeal to the viewer's reason or emotion? How does it make you feel?
   The scene is intended to create pity for Jamal because he is being tortured by the police and the fact that he is thought to be a cheater.

2. *Individuelle Lösungen.*
   Beispielantwort:
   The director changed the plot and structure of the novel. He intertwines the quiz show with the chapters of the book in a different way. He abandons the character of Smita and instead interrupts the interview at the police station with scenes from the quiz show and from other parts of Jamal's life. The reason for changing the main protagonist's name is the length of the novel; not every chapter can be turned into scenes of the movie and thus the plot must be shortened and facts and names must be changed.

6.4 *Slumdog Millionaire*, Chapter 4: being a professional beggar

Übersicht der Unterrichtseinheit(en)

Materialien: Lektüre: *10,000 Rupees*, 83 – 112; DVD: **Kap. 4: 21:28 – 35:10**; Worksheets 23a / 23b	**Kompetenz:** Funktionale kommunikative Kompetenzen (Hör- und Sehverstehen); Leseverstehen (Lektüretext und Film) Anwendung des aktiven Wortschatzes in Diskussionsphasen	
Ablauf	**Impulse**	**Sozialform Methode**
a) WS 23a / 23b: *10,000 Rupees*	Watch the scene and take notes by filling in the grid.	EA
b) WS 23a / 23b	Arbeitsteiliges Lesen des Kapitels *10,000 Rupees* Gemeinsames Ansehen der 4. Szene des Films	GA
c) Abschlussdiskussion	Gemeinsamkeiten und Unterschiede zwischen Film und Lektüre werden thematisiert und beurteilt.	Unterrichtsgespräch

Sachanlayse / Didaktische Anmerkungen

Das Kapitel *10,000 Rupees* wurde für die Verfilmung publikumswirksam verändert. In der Lektüre werden Thomas und Salim von Maman, dem Anführer der Kinderbettler, aus einem Waisenhaus geholt, wo sie sich auch kennen gelernt haben und Freunde geworden sind. Im Film schlagen die Brüder Jamal und Salim als Müllsammler durch und werden von Maman aus dieser Situation „gerettet". Die Rettung der Jungen vor ihrem Schicksal bekommt im Film eine völlig andere Aussage. Können sie in der Lektüre zwar vor dem sexuellen Missbrauch durch den Heimleiter entfliehen, so werden sie doch durch Maman weiter misshandelt. Im Film hingegen tritt Maman als Messias auf, der den Kindern Unterschlupf und Verpflegung gewährt; das Betteln ist eine Art Dank der Kinder für diese Fürsorge. Den SuS muss bei der Bearbeitung dieser Szene deutlich werden, wie sehr die Handlung verändert wurde und warum der Regisseur des Films sich für diese Veränderungen entschieden hat. Beispielsweise wird die Blendung des kleinen Jungen in der Lektüre nie erwähnt, die Jungen vermuten, dass Maman dieses vorhat. Im Film wird die Blendung nahezu en detail gezeigt.

Das betreffende Kapitel der Lektüre wird arbeitsteilig gelesen, nachdem die SuS die Filmszenen angeschaut und mit dem Worksheet 22 die Eingangsszene bearbeitet haben. Gruppenweise wird der Film mit der Lektürevorlage verglichen. Die Ergebnisse der SuS werden auf dem Worksheet 23a bzw. 23b festgehalten und entweder von den SuS handschriftlich an die Tafel gebracht oder von der Lehrkraft auf eine Overheadfolie kopiert und so dem Plenum zur Diskussion zur Verfügung gestellt. Als Ergebnissicherung sollte eine Übersicht erstellt werden, etwa in Form einer Mindmap, welche die Veränderungen von Lektüre zu Film darstellen und begründen. Wenn möglich, sollte in dieser Unterrichtsphase ein Fernseher oder Computer bzw. Laptop mit Kopfhörern zur Verfügung stehen, um den SuS zu ermöglichen, die entsprechenden Szenen noch einmal anzuschauen, um ihre Notizen und die Unterschiede zu überprüfen.

VI. Module 5: The Movie

Mögliche Lösungen für Worksheets 23a bzw. 23b

Group 1: **93** 6 – **96** 27

Novel	Film	Reason for Difference
Thomas and Salim are "adopted" by Maman as the warden of the juvenile home. In fact, he sells them to Maman, who takes them to Mumbai by train. The boys feel great and believe in a better future because they are told they are being sent to a music school.	Jamal and Salim are working as rubbish sorters together with Latika when Maman visits the rubbish dump, offers a few children a cold drink and takes them home with him.	The film director needed to place the children in a different environment because of the new character, Latika, who would not have been able to be with the boys in a juvenile home. Another reason for the difference is that Maman looks even more like a saviour when he takes them away from the rubbish dump.

Group 2: **97** – **101** 14

Novel	Film	Reason for Difference
When they arrive at Maman's house, a school for crippled children, the accommodation and the food are a lot better than in the juvenile home. All of the other boys are crippled or malformed, Thomas and Salim seem to be the only ones who are healthy. Thomas and Salim have their first singing lesson and Thomas turns out to be a bad singer.	Jamal and Salim enjoy a meal with the other children, who are not all crippled or malformed. There are boys and girls and even a baby. In their first singing lesson, Salim becomes Maman's helper, because Maman is impressed by his bravery. Salim is the one who can't sing well and from now on works as Maman's bloodhound who controls and punishes the children; while in the book Salim has a tender heart, his character in the movie is cruel and cold-blooded even towards his own brother.	The director needed to turn Salim into Maman's bloodhound so he could make him a criminal as an adult in the movie. Therefore Salim needed to be the bad singer and Thomas the one in danger of being blinded. Salim is only kind as a child; later on as an adolescent he will be egoistical and cruel.

Group 3: **101** 15 – **106** 12

Novel	Film	Reason for Difference
Thomas and Salim find out that the school they were to go to doesn't exist; they are to become beggars. They talk to different children and find out that their fate seems to be final; they have to give all their money to Maman, they have no chance of making a living in Mumbai if they run away because the gangs run the city and nobody is allowed to live and work in a different gang's area.	The fate of the child beggars is shown differently; while the novel only tells of the negative sides, the film shows not only the bad sides, such as bad treatment of the children by Maman, his helpers and Salim, but also happy times e.g. when the other children take revenge by putting chillies into Salim's bed.	While the novel criticizes the existence of child beggars, the film does not. The text of the novel is changed into a more sensational screenplay for better entertainment. Audiences are shocked by pictures of filth and misery, then "comforted" when Jamal and Salim manage to escape.

Group 4: **106** 13 – **111** 3

Novel	Film	Reason for Difference
Thomas and Salim overhear a conversation between Maman and another gangster, in which they say that Salim is "ready" and that they will "do" him and Thomas tonight. Thomas becomes suspicious and convinces Salim that they have to leave; they run away and get on a train where they meet various child beggars. They meet a blind one and give him a 100 Rupee note they found at Maman's.	The blinding of a boy is shown and even the cold-blooded Salim is shocked by what is done to the child. Even though he has been cruel towards his brother, he now saves him from mutilation and runs away with him and Latika. Latika stays behind.	There is no hint in the novel that the children are blinded by Maman. Thomas only suspects that something terrible is going to happen to them because he knows that crippled children earn more money as beggars. The director wanted to produce a film with wide public appeal and thus turned Thomas' suspicion into action by showing the blinding of a young boy. That Latika accompanies the boys' flight is necessary for the further development of the film's plot: Jamal will search for his lost love until he finds her.

Module 1: The life of an Indian orphan

Orphans

Tasks:
1. *Look at the picture (called Orphans) and describe it in detail.*
2. *Interpret the picture, taking the following aspects into consideration:*
   - *the painter's intention / the painting's message*
   - *how he conveys his intention through the picture*
   - *the effect on the viewer*
   - *your personal opinion about how the painter managed to transport his message through the picture*

Module 1: The life of an Indian orphan — WS 1b

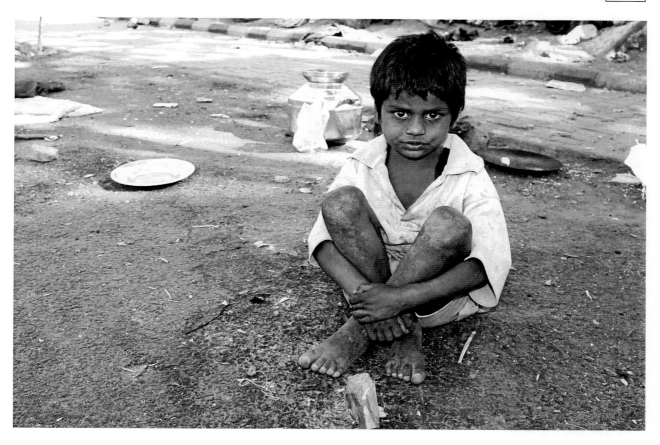

Tasks:

1. Look at this photo of an orphan in India and describe it in detail.
2. Interpret the picture taking the following aspects into consideration:
    - the photographer's intention / the painting's message
    - how he conveys his intention through the picture
    - the effect on the viewer
    - your personal opinion about how the photographer managed to transport his message through the photo

WS 2a Module 1: The life of an Indian orphan

A "job" for an orphan: child beggar

Get together in groups and work on the following task.

1a. Read the chapter: *10,000 Rupees and make curriculum vitae (CVs) for Thomas and Salim.*

1b. With the help of the CV, write their biographies and describe their characters. What are Thomas and Salim really like?

Model CV

	Thomas	**Salim**
Personal Information Name: Address(es) House number, street name, postcode, city, country: Telephone: E-mail: Nationality: Date of birth:		
Education and training (school, foreign languages)		
Work experience		
Additional information / interests		
Future Plans work in… / as…		

Module 1: The life of an Indian orphan — WS 2b

2. Draw an organization chart of Maman's child beggar business. Use the back of this sheet if necessary.

Get together in groups and work on ONE of the following tasks.

3. Thomas can write. Choose one of the crippled children who told him his story and make Thomas write a letter home to the child's parents asking for help.

or

4. Write a letter to a welfare organisation asking for help. Your letter has to be quite "aggressive" if you want to convince them that you out of a million orphans need their help!

_____

_____

_____

_____

_____

_____

_____

_____

Prepare a poster, PPT presentation or presentation on an overhead projector.

Module 1: The life of an Indian orphan — WS 3a

Slums

1. Brainstorm on which adjectives best describe a slum and write them in this box:

2. Choose the ONE which you think is the most appropriate.
3. Look at the photos and discuss whether the adjectives that you collected are appropriate. Discuss with a partner or in groups which adjectives you think are the most appropriate.
4. Write a short text describing a day in a slum. Use the photos for inspiration.

5. Read the chapter: 5,000 Rupees and talk with a partner or in a group. Compare the description of Thomas' and Salim's life in the slum with your description. Find differences and similarities.
6. Comment on the author's "stream of consciousness" technique on **78** 22 – **79** 30.

Module 1: The life of an Indian orphan

Module 1: The life of an Indian orphan

Module 1: The life of an Indian orphan WS 4

Welfare organisations in India

You are going to prepare a presentation about welfare organisations in India that try to improve orphans' living conditions and futures.

Get together in groups of four and search the Internet for an organisation you'd like to present. Then work on some or all of the following aspects:

1. Name of organisation, date of foundation, sponsor, assignments
2. Projects for orphans and in more detail:
   a. what those projects are
   b. where they are located in India
   c. how many children live there, accommodation, education of children
   d. what is done for the children's future when they have to leave the project
   e. how the organisation is financed
   f. what former residents think of the organisation

Use the website as a source of information. If you have any questions, don't hesitate to send an email to the organisation, asking for further details. Make sure to sort out unnecessary information and to only use pictures that are important! Don't overload your presentation; keep it informative, interesting and easy to understand!

Use this space for your notes:

Child labour in India

Child labour is done by any working child who is under the age specified by law. The word, "work" means full time commercial work to sustain self or add to the family income. Child labour is a hazard to a child's mental, physical, social, educational, emotional and spiritual development. Broadly, any child who is employed in activities to feed him or herself and family is being subjected to "child labour".

Officially, there are 13 million children worldwide that work. But the actual number is much higher. India has the dubious distinction of being the nation with the largest number of child labourers in the world. 12.6 million children work in India (according to the Indian Government in 2011), UNICEF estimates there are 35 million child labourers, while 20 – 40% of child labour is domestic work. In India, a staggering 14.4 percent of all 10 to 14-year-old children are in full-time employment.

The child labourers earn little and struggle to make enough to feed themselves and their families. They do not go to school; more than half of them are unable to read and write. Poverty is one of the main reasons behind this phenomenon because child labour is a source of income for poor families. In some cases, the study found that a child's income accounted for between 34 and 37 percent of the total household income. Some children are subjected to bonded labour which means that the children work in conditions of servitude in order to pay the family's debts. The debt that binds them to their employer is incurred not by the children themselves but by their parents. The creditors (employers) "offer" these loans to destitute parents in order to secure the labour of these children. The arrangements between the parents and contracting agents are usually informal and unwritten. The number of years required to pay off such a loan is indeterminate. Inadequate schools, a lack of schools, or even the expense of schooling leaves some children with little else to do but work. The attitudes of parents also contribute to child labour; some parents feel that children should work in order to develop skills useful in the job market, instead of taking advantage of a formal education.

Child Domestic Workers are children who work within homes outside their own family, doing domestic chores such as cleaning, cooking, and running errands for their employer for payment in money or kind. 86% of child domestic workers are girls, who can be as young as ten. The children are placed in households by agents or their own families. This is particularly prevalent amongst girls; it is common for a girl to work in a household at a very young age. Children placed in households by agents sometimes even have to give their salaries to agents and are thus not even able to support their family. Another sad fact is that one third of the families don't even know where their daughters are working.

---

1 **specified** made precise (*festgelegt*)
2 **commercial** for profit –
3 to **sustain** maintain, continue
8 **dubious** ['djuːbiəs] uncertain, unconvincing
12 **staggering** very surprising, shocking
17 **phenomenon** observable fact
21 **servitude** slavery
22 **to incur** to invite, to bring upon yourself
24 **destitute** very poor, impoverished
27 **indeterminate** [ˌɪndɪˈtɜːmɪnət] undefined
27 **inadequate** insufficient, not enough
28 **expense** cost
33 **chores** [tʃɔːz] everyday jobs
34 **kind** here: something similar (*Naturalien*)
37 **prevalent** common, usual
39 **salary** wage

The working conditions of child domestic workers are inhumane, too. Working days can be as long as 15 hours; often there is less than one hour break a day and no holidays to see their families; they are isolated from
45 other children; sometimes they have to ask for permission for food, any many children are underfed and more likely to be ill than when they were at home; most of them earn less than €13 a month (Rs. 1000 – 1500) and 77% have not had a wage increase in the last two years. In addition, child domestic workers face all kinds of abuse – physical, emotional and sexual.
50 The Indian government has long hesitated to employ strict rules against child labour. In 1973 the ILO (International Labour Organisation) passed laws that stipulated that no child below the minimum school leaving age, which is 15. But developing countries are allowed to set the minimum age at 14 years in accordance with their socio- economic
55 circumstances. So there was the possibility for flexibility for certain countries, which set a minimum age as low as 12 – if only for doing light work. Light work can be defined as that which does not damage health and development or interfere with education. It is because of this that many children employed in part time work time (3 – 4 hours) after school,
60 are not called child labourers. In 1990 India signed agreements at the Convention on the Rights of the Child (CRC) which bound them to ban child labour. Sadly, though, child labour still remains unpunishable by law in India.

In 2004 the Indian government set the minimum age of employment
65 at 15, including domestic work. But as of 2011, no laws for the punishment of those that contravene this had been passed.

46 **underfed** malnourished, starving
48 **increase** rise (more money)
50 **to hesitate** to be indecisive
52 **stipulated** fixed
58 **to interfere** to get in the way

Sources: the Azad India Foundation (www.azadindia.org) and Save the Children (www.savethechildren.org.uk) websites

Tasks:

1. Read the text and summarize it in your own words.

2. Give your opinion about the present state of child labour.

3. Comment on the Taylor's practice of employing Thomas at the age of 14.

4. Point out the reasons why child labour in 3rd world countries today is so common.

5. Write an open letter to the Indian government asking them to finally pass laws that criminalize child labour.

Module 2: The lives of the whites in India

Racial attacks in Australia: why only Indians?

by Om Prakash Yadav

2 **rabid** [ˈræbɪd] extreme
2 **menace** [ˈmenɪs] threat, danger
3 **condemnation** Verdammnis
15 **simplistic** naïve
15 **to brand** to identify
16 **opportunistic** taking immediate advantage, often unethically, of any circumstance of possible benefit
20 **vestigial** [vesˈtɪdʒɪəl] leaving a visible trace or evidence of something
22 **ostensible** apparent
22 **chagrin** [ˈʃæɡrɪn] embarrassment, sorrow
22 **to prevail** exist
23 **to lament** to express grief for or about; mourn
23 **vociferous** loud
25 **astounding** amazing
29 **wrangle noisy or** angry quarrel; bickering
31 **to torment to** torture
31 **lackadaisical** [ˌlækəˈdeɪzɪkl] careless, lazy
31 **callous** [ˈkæləs] very cruel
38 **inferiority complex** Minderwertigkeitskomplex

The recent attacks on Indian students studying in Australia have attracted global attention. This rabid cultural and racial menace has attracted worldwide condemnation. Sravan Kumar Theerthala was hit with petrol bottles by some unidentified teens while he was reading a
5 book in his house at Melbourne. Baljinder Singh, another student from India studying in Melbourne, was robbed and stabbed in his abdomen. Both are struggling for their lives in hospitals. Sravan's condition is reported to be very critical, he is still in coma.

In a separate incident, four students were attacked and burgled by
10 racist elements in Australia. [...] According to student's organisations, these racist attacks have been taking place in Australia for quite some time; most of them went unreported. According to a report, about 20 racial attacks on Indians took place last month in Sydney alone. [...]

The incidents have raised the question for the reasons of such attacks.
15 It is too simplistic a proposition to categorically brand them as acts of criminal or opportunistic activities, as claimed by Australian High Commissioner, John McCarthy. He has, however, not denied that some racist elements might have been involved in what he called "shameful criminal acts". [...]

20 It seems that the existence of these vestigial racial elements even in cultural, plural societies does have other hidden reasons apart from ostensible causes. Chagrin does not prevail in Australia; and even the Australian media lamented only after vociferous diplomatic and societal protests at home.

25 India has written stories of astounding success in economic fields; thanks to brilliant young brains in fields of science and technology, management and other frontier areas, who have studied in universities outside of India. [...] The student community particularly does not like to be involved in legal wrangles because they think that they have come
30 here not to fight legal battles but to complete their studies and make careers. They are also tormented by the lackadaisical, callous and sometimes ignorant attitude of police. For instance, in Australia, the police did not act till the matter was so public that they had to. [...]

Progress and affluence of students studying abroad do become visible
35 in their lifestyles. This, sadly, tempts racist elements to attack them, sometimes physically. This serves a twin purpose for the attackers; firstly they steal from the rich students, and secondly it serves their hidden inferiority complexes.

Reprinted by kind permission of Merinews.com

Tasks:

1. Read the text and sum up the author's reasons for racist attacks on Indian students in Australia.
2. Comment on the author's reasons.

Australia – racist towards Indians?

Feb 10 2010

NEW DELHI: Worried by the damage to its reputation in India and bilateral ties, Australia has now acknowledged that some of the attacks on Indians in the recent past were racial in nature, and promised to punish those responsible.

The admission came from Australian foreign minister Steven Smith in a speech in Parliament on Tuesday on Australia-India relations where he also said that the "contemptible" and "inexcusable" attacks have lowered Australia's esteem in India while casting a shadow over bilateral ties.

"If any of these attacks have been racist in nature – and it seems clear some of them have – they will be punished with the full force of the law," said Smith. […].

Smith's speech, in which he asserted that his country had zero tolerance for terrorism, fully brought out Australia's anxiety about the fallout of the racist attacks on ties with India, which he called a country with a growing global role.

"Recent contemptible attacks on Indian students and others of Indian origin in Australia have cast a long shadow, not only over our education links, but across our broader relationship and bilateral agenda. These attacks are inexcusable," said the Australian foreign minister. […] There was a need to work with diligence and dedication to extend the partnership. "The era of inactivity and even neglect is over," he added, while emphasising India's growing global role, the strategic relationship between both countries and the future trajectory of bilateral relations.

Smith stressed that Australia had emerged as a major destination for Indian students studying abroad. Enrolment had gone up at an average annual rate of over 40% since 2002. Currently there were over 120,000 Indian students. The Australian foreign minister also said that the education and visa system for international students in Australia was being reformed to ensure only genuine students applied. "We have increased to $18,000 per year the amount that international students must prove they have to support themselves financially before they can obtain a student visa," said Smith.

Detailing the measures undertaken by Prime Minister Kevin Rudd's government, Smith said the law enforcement agencies had brought perpetrators of attacks to justice. In Victoria State alone, Smith said, 45 people had been arrested for crimes against Indian students or nationals. Almost half of Indian students in Australia study in Victoria.

Following the attacks, Smith acknowledged that repairing the Australian brand and reputation in India was an essential priority. "Just as Australia and Australians need to recognise the realities of India's evolving society and emergence as a global influence, we have to work harder to convey to India and Indians an appreciation of contemporary Australia," he said, adding that immigration was very important for Australia's economic and social success.

Article found at: http://articles.timesofindia.indiatimes.com/2010-02-10/india/28116225_1_student-visa-bilateral-ties-australia-india

---

2 **bilateral** [baɪˈlætrl] **two-sided**
5 **admission** *Geständnis*
7 **contemptible** disgraceful, shameful
8 **esteem** regard, respect
12 **to assert** to declare, to state
13 **anxiety** [æŋˈzaɪəti] **nervousness**, worry
18 **links** associates
20 **diligence** [ˈdɪlɪdʒəns] thoroughness
20 **dedication** devotion, commitment
21 **neglect** abandon, carelessness
23 **trajectory** [trəˈdʒektri] course, (here) plans
25 **enrolment** *Einschreibung als Student in einer Universität*
29 **genuine** [ˈdʒenjuɪn] *here:* real students, not people who come to Australia to look for asylum
31 **to obtain** to get
34 **perpetrator** person who is responsible for sth
39 **to evolve** to develop, to change
40 **to convey** to express, to put across
41 **appreciation** approval, admiration
41 **contemporary** current

Task:

Read the text and comment on the Australian foreign minister's way of apologising for the attacks.

Police Violence

"No this isn't 'the old good cop, bad cop routine'. This is the old bad cop, worst cop routine!"

© CartoonStock Ltd

Tasks:

1. Look at the cartoon and describe it in detail.
2. Summarise the cartoonist's message. Explain how he uses symbols and words to transport this message.
3. Comment on the cartoon and on the way it criticizes the problem of police violence.
4. Look at the picture and think of a title for it.

Police violence in India

Deaths in judicial custody between 2000 and 2008

Year	No. of deaths	percentage increase
2000 – 2001	910	
2001 – 2002	1,140	25,25
2002 – 2003	1,157	27,14
2003 – 2004	1,300	42,86
2004 – 2005	1,357	49,12
2005 – 2006	1,591	74,84
2006 – 2007	1,477	62,31
2007 – 2008	1,789	96,59
Overall	**8,932**	**54,92**

Deaths in police custody between 2000 and 2009

Year	No. of deaths	percentage increase
2000 – 2001	127	
2001 – 2002	165	29,92
2002 – 2003	183	44,09
2003 – 2004	162	27,56
2004 – 2005	136	7,09
2005 – 2006	139	9,45
2006 – 2007	119	-6,30
2007 – 2008	187	47,24
2008 – 2009	127	0
Totals:	**1,345**	**19,88**

Tasks:

1. Look at the statistics.
2. Interpret them with the help of WS 9b "Analysing statistics"
3. Make a graph (or several graphs) that you think best conveys the message or messages of these statistics.
4. Sum up the meaning of each graph in one sentence.

Analysing tables

Numbers and statistics can serve several purposes: to present raw data, to show developments over a period of time, to compare different aspects (quantities, amounts, size, etc'). They can be presented in many different ways such as tables, line graphs, pie charts, bar charts' etc.

When you work with statistics you have to consider the following 6 steps in your analysis:

1. Mention the source of the numbers and the topic after looking at the title and the legend. How reliable might the statistics be? Are the numbers up-to-date?
2. Explain the formal components of the presentation such as period of time, columns, curves, horizontal and vertical lines, percentages, absolute numbers, quantities, etc.
3. Study the statistics and read all the information about a chart carefully. Are the numbers you see absolute numbers or percentages? The title or the legend (i.e. the information next to the graph) will usually tell you this.
4. Describe the contents and details such as changes and developments over time, peak and low points, relationships and connections.
5. Draw a conclusion from the numbers. If conclusions are drawn from statistics, think carefully. Is the conclusion given really what the numbers suggest? Are there other possible interpretations?
6. You should also be critical about the form of presentation: e.g. Is it in an easily understandable form? Is it from a reliable source? Are the numbers up-to-date? What is your objective – balanced information or to manipulate the results?

Useful phrases for the analysis of statistics

This table shows / is about / provides information about …
In the first column, …
On the horizontal line, there is …
The vertical line represents …
The chart consists of …
The percentage of … is very small / large
The majority of …
Nearly half of …
Compared to …, you can see a huge decrease …
There is a slight rise (in) …
to rise / increase
to decrease / drop
X remained constant / reached a low / peak / an all-time high
This clearly indicates that …

Module 3: The dark side of India WS 10

India – Crime rates

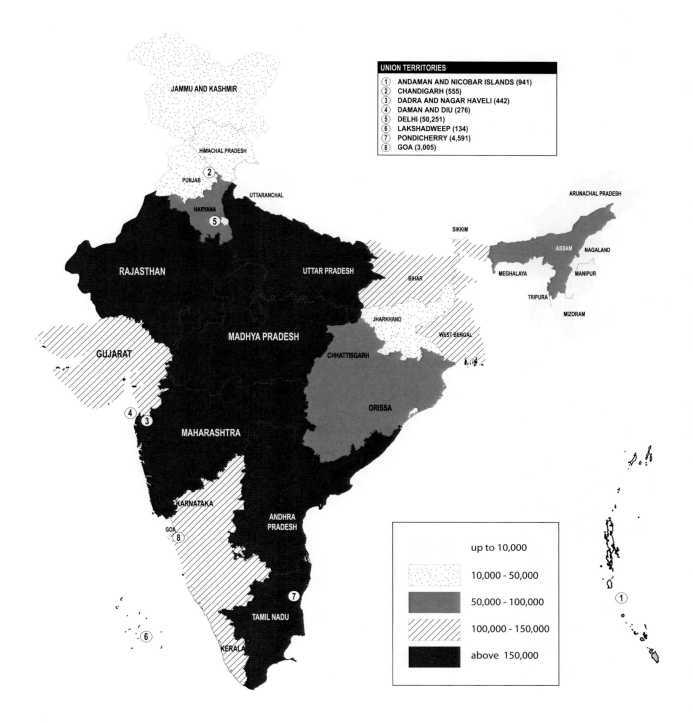

Tasks:

1. Describe in detail what is shown on the map. Interpret the statistics.

2. Make a list of all the crimes committed in Slumdog Millionaire. Compare this list to the crime rates presented in the map above. Summarize your conclusions.

Crime in India and Germany

1. Arunachal Pradesh (2010)

Type of crime	TOTAL
Murder	75
Attempted Murder	34
Rape	47
Kidnapping / Abduction	67
grievous bodily harm[1]	196
criminal assault[2]	246
assault to pub servant	53
grievous bodily harm to women	119
fatal accident	106
non-fatal accident	171
riot	32
dacoity[3]	15
robbery	69
burglary	211
theft	445
extortion	113
criminal breach of trust[4]	59
other Indian Police Service cases	387
illegal sale of arms	16
illegal use and distribution of narcotics	49
minor offenses	48
TOTAL	**2558**

Quelle: www.india.gov.in

2. Germany (2009)

Straftatenanteile an "Straftaten insgesamt – 6.054.330 Fälle

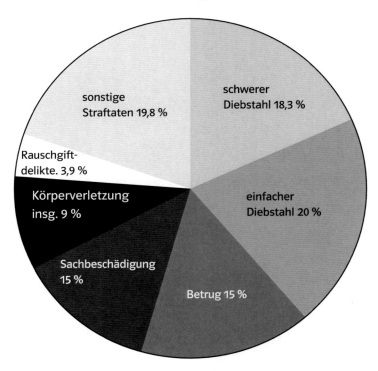

Jahrbuch 2009 (S.31), der Polizeilichen Kriminalstatistik

Tasks:

1. Work with a partner. Turn the numbers of the grid (Arunchal Pradesh) into a pie chart.
2. Look at the second pie chart about the crime statistics in Germany and compare it with the Indian statistics.
3. Find reasons for similarities and differences.
4. Relate the graph of the Indian figures to the contents of the novel.

1 **grievous bodily harm** schwere Körperverletzung – 2 **criminal assault** leichte Körperverletzung – 3 **dacoity** bandenmäßiger Raub – 4 **criminal breach of trust** Unterschlagung

Module 3: The dark side of India WS 12

Corruption – a cartoon

Found at: http://www.indiatalkies.com/2011/03/dandi-march-corruption-india.html

Tasks:

1. Look at the cartoon and describe it in detail.

2. Write a headline for the cartoon.

3. Comment on the cartoon's message.

Module 3: The dark side of India

2 **to survey** [sə'veɪ] to examine
3 **to be bracketed** to be grouped, categorized
5 **business consultancy** *Unternehmensberatung*
22 **to be wracked** made uneasy, shaken
22 **scam** trick, rip-off
27 **underway** in progress
29 **graft** *Bestechung*
36 **to underscore** to underline, to highlight

India among the most corrupt nations surveyed by PERC

Singapore, March 29, 2011

India finds itself bracketed with countries like the Philippines and Cambodia, rated as the fourth most corrupt nation among 16 countries of the Asia Pacific region surveyed by leading Hong Kong-based business consultancy firm PERC. The Political & Economic Risk Consultancy Ltd (PERC) rated India at 8.67 on a scale of zero to 10 – with the high end being the worst case of corruption scenario – and ahead of the Philippines (8.9 points), Indonesia (9.25 points) and Cambodia (9.27 points). Among the 16 countries reviewed in its latest report, Thailand was rated eleventh, with a scale of 7.55, followed by China (7.93) and Vietnam (8.3). In comparison, Singapore was given a clean sheet with a score of 0.37, followed by Hong Kong (1.10), Australia (1.39), Japan (1.90) and USA (2.39), putting them in the top five. In India, according to the report, civil and other local-level political leaders were found more corrupt than the national-level political leaders, with the former given a score of 9.25 and the latter slightly better at 8.97. Indian civil servants at the city level too were rated at 8.18, worse than the civil servants at the national level (7.76).

"The issue of corruption has grown and overshadowed the second term in office of the Congress-led coalition headed by Prime Minister Manmohan Singh," said PERC in its Asian Intelligence report on Asian business and politics. The government has been wracked by a series of scandals involving the sale of telecom licenses, preparations for the Commonwealth Games, a land scam involving high level military officers, and improper property loans made by state-owned financial institutions, it pointed out.

Though investigations were underway, to be followed by court trials, Indians were still questioning whether or not the prime minister has the political muscle to fight graft and whether the actions now being taken were more for show than proof that the government was really cracking down on business practices that were common but corrupt, it said.

Prime Minister Singh has been put in such a defensive position that most of his recent statements have been to stress how he has not personally been involved with corruption, even though it appears that almost everyone around him was, observed PERC. "This point is underscored by a recent WikiLeaks report that the ruling Congress Party paid off parliamentarians back in 2008 to pass the US-India civil nuclear deal," it said. The report also noted that the Federation of Indian Chambers of Commerce and Industry was worried that the problem of corruption and the way it was being treated in the media could seriously hurt India's international image and scare away potential investors.

It takes two to tango and the level of corruption in the public sector would not be possible if there were not plenty of private businessmen willing to pay bribes and work the political system, said PERC.

Article found at: http://www.hindustantimes.com/StoryPage/Print/679258.aspx

Tasks:

1. Read the text and turn the numbers mentioned into a bar chart.
2. Comment on the numbers in your chart, giving possible reasons for the high rates of corruption in Asian countries.

Module 3: The dark side of India

Graft is becoming a bigger problem – and the government should tackle it

Indians' anger over rising corruption has reached feverish levels. What people are calling a "season of scams" includes the alleged theft of billions by officials behind last year's Commonwealth games in Delhi; $40 billion in revenues lost from the crooked sale of 2G telecoms licences; and over $40 billion stolen in Uttar Pradesh alone from schemes subsidising food and fuel for the poor. Foreign businessmen, who have slashed investment over the past year, rank graft as their biggest headache behind appalling infrastructure. Now India's anti-corruption chief has been forced out over, well, corruption.

Graft is hardly new in India: the Bofors scandal brought down the government in 1989. But there seems to be more of it about than ever, if only because India is getting richer fast, and the faster the economy grows, the more chances arise for mind-boggling theft. The government says that in the next five-year plan period, which starts next year, $1 trillion will be spent on roads, railways, ports and so on, with billions more on re-equipping the armed forces and welfare. Add in an insatiable appetite for scarce land, water and minerals and a monsoon of bribes is forecast.

Some are inclined to shrug their shoulders. After all, corruption does not seem to be stopping India from growing. Yet imagine how much better the country would be doing without it. Corruption raises costs not just to Indians, but also to the foreigners whose capital India needs. Thanks in part to those scandals, India's stockmarket was the worst-performing outside the Muslim world over the past year.

To its credit, the government has begun to take action against powerful individuals. Maharashtra state's chief minister was forced out over a property scandal. Police have quizzed Suresh Kalmadi, the politician who ran the Commonwealth games. Most strikingly, Andimuthu Raja, the cabinet minister who oversaw the 2G telecom licences, was arrested.

A 2005 act giving the right to information is welcome, as are auctions for public goods, such as last year's lucrative sale of the 3G telecom spectrum. Technology is helping. In some states, bids for state contracts are being run online, allowing anti-corruption bodies to monitor them. Gujarat does this for all contracts over 500,000 rupees ($11,000). It also puts land records and death certificates online, cutting down on one form of graft. Websites reveal the cost of graft by publicising the sums demanded for everything from registering a baby to fixing a broken water supply.

The central government should now implement a plan for a universal, computerised ID scheme. It would allow welfare payments to be paid into individuals' bank accounts, hindering theft by state workers.

Most of all, India must redouble its efforts to liberalise. The state could outsource official tasks, cut red tape and sell wasteful and corrupt state-owned firms. Regulations are not, by and large, deterrents to corruption, but a source of it.

© The Economist Newspaper Limited, London (March 10, 2011)

2 **to tackle sth** to fight against sth
6 **crooked** ['krʊkɪd] not straight, dishonest
7 **to subsidise** to support, to pay for
8 **to slash** to cut, to gash
9 **appalling** awful, dreadful, horrible
12 **Bofors scandal** Bofors is a Swedish arms (weapons) manufacturer; the Indian Prime Minister accepted bribes from them so that they got the deal to supply weapons to the Indian army.
18 **insatiable** [ɪnˈseɪʃəbl] very greedy
31 **act** new law
39 **to implement** to put into practice
41 **to hinder** to hold back
43 **red tape** Bürokratie

Tasks:

1. Read the text and give reasons for the high rate of corruption in India according to the text.
2. Explain how India is trying to fight corruption and comment on these efforts.

Module 4: The media in India: Bollywood movies and international TV

The Genre of Bollywood movies

Bollywood is the informal name given to the popular Mumbai-based film industry in India. Its output is considered to be the largest in the world in terms of the number of films produced and, possibly, tickets sold. Bollywood is a very important part of popular culture of India and the rest of the Indian subcontinent. The word *Bollywood* was created by blending *Bombay* (the city now officially called Mumbai) and *Hollywood*.

Bollywood films are usually musicals; very few movies are made without at least one song-and-dance number. Indian audiences expect full value for their money: songs and dances, love triangles, comedy and dare-devil thrills – all are mixed up in a three hour long extravaganza with an intermission. Plots tend to be melodramatic and frequently employ standard ingredients such as star-crossed lovers and angry parents, corrupt politicians, kidnappers, conniving villains, courtesans with hearts of gold, long-lost relatives and siblings separated by fate, dramatic reversals of fortune, and convenient coincidences. Sex scenes are censored and kissing is rare in traditional Bollywood movies.

There have always been films with more "artistic" aims and more sophisticated stories. They often lost out at the box office to movies with more mass appeal. The props in the films are often very grand. There are elaborate costumes such as traditional saris and dresses. Other characteristics that are commonly associated with Bollywood films are the dominance of the hero and the heroine and the presence of a religious figure that all the characters believe in, such as a god or deity.

While most actors, especially today, are excellent dancers, few are also singers. Songs are generally pre-recorded by professional playback singers with actors lip-synching the words, often while dancing. Playback singers are prominently featured in the opening credits and have their own fans. The dancing in Bollywood films, especially older ones, is primarily modelled on Indian dance: classical dance styles, dances of historic northern Indian courtesans or folk dances. The hero or heroine will often perform with a troupe of supporting dancers, usually of the same sex. If the hero and heroine dance and sing a pas-de-deux, it is often staged in beautiful natural surroundings or architecturally grand settings.

---

2 **output** amount produced
5 **to blend** to combine
10 **dare devil** Teufelskerl, Tausendsassa
10 **to slash** to cut, to gash
11 **extravaganza** big, very entertaining show
11 **intermission** break
11 **melodramatic** overdramatic
12 **star-crossed** ill-fated, unlucky
13 **conniving** manipulative
13 **courtesan** Kurtisane, Mätresse
14 **siblings** Geschwister
15 **reversal** turnaround
15 **coincidence** twist of fate
18 **sophisticated** advanced
18 **box office** Kinokasse
19 **mass appeal:** mass attraction
19 **props** Requisiten
20 **elaborate** sophisticated
23 **deity** Gottheit
27 **to be featured** to be named
31 **troupe** group
32 **pas-de-deux** two people dancing together
32 **to be staged** to be set
33 **surroundings** environment

Tasks:

1. Read the text and take notes on the characteristics of a Bollywood movie.

2. Name differences to Western (Hollywood or European productions) movies.

Heroes and heroines of Bollywood movies

1. Fill in the grid.

A Bollywood Hero	A Bollywood heroine
First impression:	**First impression:**
purpose / aim of photographer:	purpose / aim of photographer:
personal opinion about photo:	personal opinion about photo:

Module 4: The media in India: Bollywood movies and international TV — WS 17b

2. Get together in groups. Read chapter 1,000 Rupees: Death of a Hero or 10,000,000 Rupees: Tragedy Queen.

3. Describe the character of either Armaan Ali or Neelima Kumari based on the text of the novel and fill in the mind-map with your findings.

4. Taking the fact into consideration that both Ali's and Kumar's career have ended – Ali's due to his homosexuality and Kumar's because of her suicide – write an obituary for him or her.

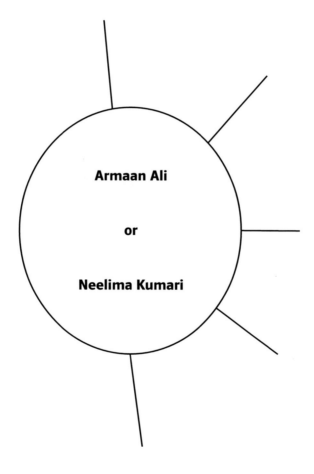

Module 4: The media in India: Bollywood movies and international TV / Klausur

Indian women – Heroine, prostitute, worker

Women in India

India is a country of discrepancies. Even though the Indian constitution guarantees the equal treatment of men and women, extreme disproportions are still common. Women traditionally live the traditional life of a mother and wife. Women's roles were laid down in Hindu law books such as the *Laws of*
5 *Manu*. Nevertheless women's roles have evolved over time and some women do not conform to the social norm. Women are portrayed in sacred scriptures as possessing a duality, being both benevolent and malevolent, thus having greatly contrasting powers. Women should remain passive, running the household, rearing the children, and participating in religious rituals as an
10 assistant to their husband. There should be no independence and autonomy for Indian women. If the husband dies, the son is in charge of the mother and she has to obey his orders. This is the concept of Patrivrata, the wife should see her husband as a god and treat him accordingly. If her husband dies, she has to follow him by committing suicide (often by burn herself to death). Widows are
15 not allowed to remarry. In old scriptures, the purpose of the woman is also described as bearing the husband male children. Only through sons can the father's spirit live on. Therefore, the birth of a daughter was considered to be almost a tragedy. Daughters are expensive. They live in the husband's family after their marriage and don't support their own family anymore. In addition,
20 extremely high dowries are demanded by the husbands' families; this can lead to the financial ruin of the bride's family. Marriages and the amount or price of the dowries are decided by the parents, whereby the bride's parents are put under extreme social pressure because an unmarried daughter means shame for the complete family.

25 Daughters are not only expensive but it's not worth "investing" in their educations: only approximately 54 % of Indian girls attend school (2011). The rate of illiteracy of women is twice as high as that of men in India.

The dowry system is illegal, there are laws against it, but it still is common in rural India. The dowry used to consist of money, jewellery and household items,
30 now the husband's family often ask for refrigerators, washing machines, TVs, motor scooters or even cars. Sometimes the financial claims continue after the wedding. In some cases, if the family of the bride cannot meet these demands, there have been cases of "accidents" where the bride suffered a fatal injury and the husband could remarry and ask for another dowry. Dowry murders are not
35 only common in rural India but also in urban areas of the country. The Indian Government records 7,000 dowry murders per year, the estimated number of unknown cases is probably higher. Due to the dowry system and parents' fear of having to pay absurd dowry demands the future of girls is bleak. Of children age of 1 to 9, 60 % more girls die than boys. Girls are breast-fed less than boys,
40 get less and worse food and are treated medically less frequently than boys. It is not uncommon for female babies are killed right after their birth in rural areas. The middle classes often seek the help of prenatal diagnostics: about 5 million female foetuses are aborted every year according to the Indian Medical Association. According to official statistics there were only 927 girls for every

---

1 **discrepancy** difference
2 **disproportion** imbalance
5 **to evolve** to develop
7 **duality** *Dualität*
7 **benevolent** kind, giving
7 **malevolent** wicked, nasty
9 **to rear to** bring up
16 **to bear to** give birth
20 **dowry** (*pl:* dowries): *Mitgift*
27 **illiteracy** *Analphabetismus*
42 **prenatal diagnostics**
Pränataldiagnostik, Untersuchungen vor der Geburt, bei denen sowohl Krankheiten als auch das Geschlecht des Fötus festgestellt werden kann.

45 1,000 boys in 2001. This development leads to a dangerous demographic situation: no women means no (male) offspring! This imbalance leads to the development of trafficking: women from the poorest parts of India and the lowest castes have to fill the gaps on the marriage market.

Violence against women is not only normal in India but on the rise, too. About
50 every 3 minutes there is a crime against a woman, every 9 minutes a woman is raped in India, often by family members or her own husband. There are various NGOs fighting for women's rights in India, asking for more rights and self-determination.

Women like Indira Ghandi or Kalpana Chawla are rare, though there are
55 women in India working as politicians, software experts, doctors and engineers. But change only happens in big cities, in rural areas the ancient gender roles dominate; women serve their husbands and families, they walk for miles to get water or firewood and often work as day labourers, earning only half as much as men.

60 India wants to play a role in the globalised world but it is still a third-world country when it comes to women's rights.

Text by: Frauke Vieregge, 2011

47 **trafficking** abduction / resettlement of people against their will with a criminal and inhuman background
48 **caste** social group in India
52 **NGO** non-governmental organization, welfare or help organization
52 **self-determination** Selbstbestimmung

1. Read the text and explain why the dowry system is prohibited by law in India.

2. Read the chapter: 100,000,000 Rupees and make notes on the different life situations of women that are described in the text.

3. Comment on the situation of women in India today and on how this is portrayed in the novel. Find pictures of ordinary Indian women on the Internet to help you.

4. Explain why the fact that girls are of less value than boys in India might be dangerous for the country's future. If possible, refer to information about other Asian countries.

Film terminology

1. Look at the pictures.

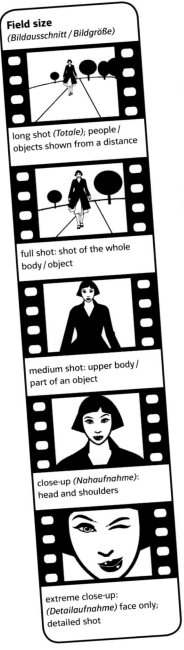
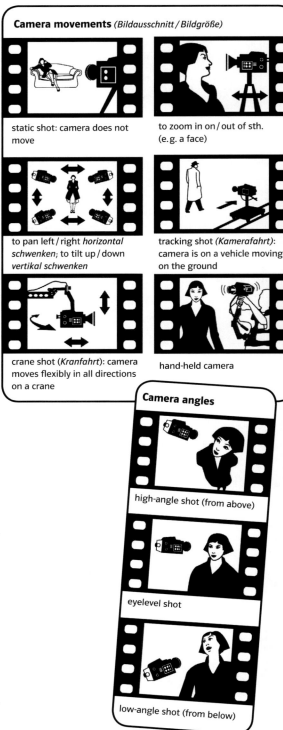

2. Choose two pictures and explain in detail why and when they might be used in a movie. Give examples of when they might be used.

_____

_____

_____

_____

Module 5: The Movie — WS 20

Elements of Film Narrative – Narration and Narrator

Who tells the story in a film?
In every film the main storyteller is the camera. Through the eyes of the camera the viewer is led through the story of the film. Even if you switch off the sound, you can still follow the basic story of the film. But, of course, to really understand the film, you have to listen to the dialogues and the narration of the film. There are different types of narration:

1. Try to explain the two most common types of narration in films (first-person and voice-over narration).

2. Give an example for each from a film of your own choice.

   a) **First-person narration**

   _____

   _____

   _____

   _____

   b) **Voice-over narration**

   _____

   _____

   _____

   _____

   c) **Direct-address narration**

   A character talks directly to the audience. (This is not done very often because it is one of the viewing conventions that there is an assumed barrier or "wall" between the characters on screen and the audience.)

Quelle: African Americans in Film, Susanne Heinz (Klett, 978-3-12-577468-1)

The Language of Films – Glossary

A film can be subdivided into smaller units:

shot: the basic unit of a film, one uninterrupted run of the camera

scene: a dramatic unit composed of one or several shots. A scene usually takes places at one point of time, in the same setting, and involves the same characters.

sequence: a larger unit of film, a series of (edited) shots which have one theme or purpose and form a coherent unit in the development of the plot

I Distance between the camera and the object

Field size	Technique	Function
extreme close-up:	camera is extremely close to sb or sth	gives particular attention
close-up:	camera is very close to the object	concentrates viewer's attention on sth or sb specific, eg feelings
medium shot:	shows person from the waist up	brings viewer closer to the action
full shot:	full view of a person (entire body) and not much else	gives viewer complete picture of sb or sth
long shot:	camera is at a great distance from the subject or object being filmed	presents an entire setting (good for viewer's orientation)

II Positions and angle of the camera

Type of shot	Camera Position / Angle	Function
establishing shot:	opening shot or sequence, usually a LS which includes a wide view of the setting	sets the scene for the coming action
eye-level shot:	shot made from the observer's eye level	gives the impression of authenticity and directness
high-angle shot / overhead shot:	camera looks down at a character	makes a character seem small, weak, vulnerable
low-angle shot:	camera is placed below the character	enlarges sth or sb, stresses its importance / power
point-of-view shot:	scene shown from character's point of view	audience identifies more closely with character
reaction shot:	shot showing a character's reaction (surprise, amusement, anger, horror)	viewer is given a character's interpretation of an object, another character or of the scene

Module 5: The Movie
WS 21b

III Camera movement

Camera Movement	Technique	Function
panning:	To pan left and right, the camera moves from left to right (horizontal movement).	eg follows a particular action; moves viewer's attention
tilt:	To tilt up and down, the camera moves up or down (vertical movement).	eg shows the subject in his/her full length
tracking shot:	camera follows or precedes an object which is in motion itself	allows viewer to move along with the action, adds speed
zoom:	the movement is done by the camera lens only without the camera itself moving	concentrates attention on sb/sth or moves attention

IV Lighting (source: natural or artificial, in most cases artificial light)

Quality of light	Technique	Function
high key lighting:	soft, even lighting, very little contrast, in extreme cases no shadows at all	softening details/a character's face, often used in romantic stories/comedies
low key lighting:	harsh, high-contrast lighting, creates dark shadows	associated with serious or tragic stories, underlines ambivalence in a character
Halloween lighting:	lighting from below a character, creates unnatural shadows in a character's face	creates a mystery/threatening effect

The interrogation - analysis

1. Watch the first scene closely and fill in the grid with your findings.

Brief description of sequence	
What happens at the level of plot or narration in this sequence?	
What role does this sequence play within the whole plot of the film (e.g. rising action, climax, turning point, exposition, character development, motifs, patterns, etc.)?	
Cinematography: Note composition, camera movement, off-screen space, colour etc.	
Note how camera angles, lighting, music, narration, and / or editing contribute to creating an atmosphere in this film.	
Does the scene appeal to the viewer's reason or emotion? How does it make you feel?	

2. Comment on the first scene of the movie, stating your opinion about how the director turned the plot of the novel into a movie.

Module 5: The Movie WS 23a

10,000 Rupees: A thought for the crippled

Get into four groups and compare the novel from **93** *6 –* **111** *13 it with the film (Chapter 4: 21:28 – 35:10).*

Group 1 (**93** 6 – **96** 27)

Novel	Film	Reason for Difference

Group 2 (**97** – **101** 14)

Novel	Film	Reason for Difference

Ws 23b Module 5: The Movie

10,000 Rupees: A thought for the crippled

Get into four groups and compare the novel from **93** *6 –* **111** *13 it with the film (Chapter 4: 21:28 – 35:10).*

Group 3 (**101** 15 – **106** 12)

Novel	Film	Reason for Difference

Group 4 (**106** 13 – **111** 3)

Novel	Film	Reason for Difference

VIII. Anhang

8.1 Brief history of modern India *(adapted from a text by Monika Plümer)*

1947	August 15th, Independence Day Partition of India into two independent nations, India and Pakistan. Punjab and Bengal divided along religious boundaries. Kashmir remains disputed. This leads to over 12 million refugees and 1 million dead in massacres between Sikhs, Hindus and Muslims.
1948	Gandhi assassinated by a Hindu fanatic
1948	War with Pakistan over the disputed territory of Kashmir
1950	Hindi officially made the national language of India, but English remains in fact the dominant language in Parliament, law, higher education, commerce and industry
1951	First general elections: Jawaharlal Nehru (Congress Party) wins and remains Prime Minister until 1964
1962	Indo-Chinese border conflict, India loses this war against China
Early 1960s	The Green Revolution and the White Revolution see India transformed from a country reliant on food aid due to chronic shortages into an exporter of food, cotton and milk.
1964	Nehru dies in office. Lal Bahadur Shastri takes over as Prime Minister, Indira Gandhi, Nehru's daughter, becomes a member of his cabinet.
1965	Pakistani infiltration into Kashmir leads to a second war with Pakistan
1966	Indira Gandhi is elected Prime Minister after Shastri's death within hours of signing a peace agreement with Ayub Khan of Pakistan.
1971	Renewed military conflict with Pakistan ends with a crushing victory for India and the formation of the independent nation of Bangladesh (formerly East Pakistan).
1971	India signs twenty-year treaty of friendship with Soviet Union
1974	India becomes a nuclear power after conducting underground tests in Rajasthan.
1975	Protests against the government, amidst claims that Gandhi's election was invalid: Indira Gandhi's emergency rule (until 1977)
1975–77	nearly 1,000 political opponents imprisoned; government introduces programme of compulsory birth control
1977	Morarji Desai (Janata Party) becomes Prime Minister after Gandhi's Congress Party is defeated.
1979	Charan Singh (Janata Party) becomes Prime Minister after Desai's resignation
1980	Indira Gandhi returns to office as Prime Minister in a landslide victory heading Congress Party splinter group

1984	Indira Gandhi is assassinated by her own Sikh bodyguards. Her son, Rajiv, succeeds her and later wins elections.
1984	gas leak at Union Carbide pesticides plant in Bhopal in December, thousands immediately killed, many more die subsequently or are left handicapped
1989	Rajiv Gandhi defeated in general election. V.P. Singh becomes Prime Minister of minority government which includes members of Hindu nationalist Bharatiya Janata Party (BJP).
1990	Violent riots in Punjab, Assam and Kashmir. Escalation of social and sectarian violence due to Hindu nationalism and caste policies (quotas). V.P. Singh loses vote of confidence; Chandra Shekhar forms the Samajwadi Janata Dal and becomes Prime Minister, with Rajiv Gandhi's support.
1990	Indian troops withdraw from Sri Lanka Muslim separatist groups begin a campaign of violence in Kashmir
1991	Rajiv Gandhi assassinated by a LTTE (*Liberation Tigers of Tamil Eelam*) suicide bomber. P.V. Narasimha Rao (Congress) becomes Prime Minister of India
1992	December 6th: Hindu fundamentalists destroy 16th century mosque in Ayodhya, Uttar Pradesh, and reclaim the site as the birthplace of the god Ram, communal riots spread to other parts of India, most violently in Bombay
1996	Atal Behari Vajpayee (BJP, *Bharatiya Janata Party*, a Hindu nationalist party) becomes Prime Minister from mid-May until the beginning of June, when he is succeeded by H.D. Deve Gowda.
1997	Inder Kumar Gujral becomes Prime Minister.
1998	Sonia Gandhi, the Italian born widow of Rajiv Gandhi, becomes leader of the Congress Party. Vajpayee becomes Prime Minister again, and immediately resumes nuclear tests in Rajasthan, shattering any hopes of a peaceful resolution to the Kashmir crisis.
1999	Vajpayee makes historic bus trip to Pakistan to meet Premier Nawaz Sharif and to sign bilateral Lahore peace declaration
1999	Kargil War after Pakistani soldiers and Kashmiri militants cross onto the Indian side of the *Line of Control* in Kashmir
2000	India marks the birth of its 1 billionth citizen
2000	Corruption scandals come to a head when former Prime Minister Narasimha Rao is convicted for bribery
2000	President Clinton makes a ground breaking visit to improve relations between India and the US
2001	Massive earthquakes hit the state of Gujarat in January; at least 30,000 dead
2001	General Pervez Musharraf from Pakistan and Vajpayee meet for peace talks over Kashmir. The Kashmiri assembly in Srinagar is attacked in October, leaving several people dead, and the Indian Parliament in New Delhi is attacked in December.

2001	September: US lifts sanctions imposed on India and Pakistan (following nuclear tests in 1998). This change of US policy is seen as a reward for their post 9/11 support of US-led anti-terror campaign.
2001	Suicide bombers attack Dehli parliament, killing several policemen; India imposes sanctions on Pakistan to force it to take action against Kashmiri groups blamed for this attack, Indian and Pakistani troops assemble near the border
2002	India successfully tests a missile with nuclear capability off its eastern coast
2002	Gujarat: riots between fundamentalist Muslims and Hindus after 59 Hindu pilgrims are killed in a train fire; more than 1,000 people, mainly Muslims, die in the ensuing riots; officials blame the fire on Muslim mobs, government investigation in 2005 rules the fire accidental
2002	Pakistan test-fires missiles, war of diplomacy with India ensues; the US and UK urge their citizens to leave the region, diplomatic efforts to avert war continue
2002	A.P.J. Abdul Kalam, retired scientist and architect of India's missile programme, elected president
2003	At least 50 people killed in two simultaneous bomb blasts in Mumbai
2003	Diplomatic relations restored between India and Pakistan
2004	Sonia Gandhi leads the Congress Party to victory in the elections. Dr. Manmohan Singh becomes Prime Minister of India.
2004	India, with Germany, Brazil and Japan applies for permanent seat on UN Security Council
2004	Tsunami: Thousands killed in tidal waves which devastate coastal communities in the south
2005	First bus services in 60 years between Srinafar (Kashmir, India) and Muzaffarabad (Kashmir, Pakistan)
2005	Bomb kills 62 people in Delhi; little-known Kashmiri group says it is behind the attack
2006	**July**: More than 180 people killed in bomb attacks on rush-hour trains in Mumbai
2007	**May**: At least nine people killed in a bomb explosion at the main mosque in Hyderabad. Several more die in subsequent rioting. **May**: Government announces strongest economic growth figures for 20 years **December**: Benazir Bhutto assassinated two weeks before general elections in Pakistan
2008	**November**: Mumbai Terrorist Attacks: nearly 200 people killed and hundreds injured in a series of co-ordinated attacks by gunmen on the main tourist and business area of India's financial capital; India blames Pakistani militants and demands Pakistani Government take strong action. **December**: India announces suspension of peace process with Pakistan
2009	**April**: Trial of sole surviving suspect in Mumbai attacks begins
2010	**May**: Gunman of 2008 Mumbai attacks convicted of murder and waging war on India **June**: Eight Indians sentenced to two years jail each by a Bhopal court for "death by negligence" over 1984 Union Carbide gas plant leak **August**: Devastating floods in Pakistan affect almost 21 million people

8.2 Literaturverzeichnis

URLs zu Modul 1 (Online-Link: 579875-0011)
http://www.smiling-children.de/hilfsprojekte,indien,bhubaneswar-daya,de.php
http://www.unicef.org/infobycountry/india_statistics.html
http://www.gfbv.de/pressemit.php?id=2011
http://www.stern.de/politik/ausland/mail-aus-mumbai-vom-bettler-zum-millionaer-612659.html
http://www.spiegel.de/schulspiegel/ausland/0,1518,667470,00.html

URLs zu Modul 2 (Online-Link: 579875-0022)
http://www.azadindia.org/social-issues/child-labour-in-india.html
http://www.childlabor.in
http://www.savethechildren.org.uk/eyetoeye/downloads/E2E_India_work_background.ppt

URLs zu Modul 4 (Online-Link: 579875-0044)
http://mumbaimoments.com/bollywood-transition.html
http://imdb.com (Hollywood Film Poster, gratis herunterzuladen)

Buch
Andrea Glaubacker: *Indien... von Buddha bis Bollywood*: Conbook Verlag, 2009, S. 74-81